# COACHING

# Off-Broadway Basketball

# COACHING
# OFF-BROADWAY BASKETBALL

AN OPERATING MANUAL FOR NEW AND INTERESTED BASKETBALL COACHES

JOHN HURLEY

ORANGE *frazer* PRESS
*Wilmington, Ohio*

ISBN 978-1939710-734


Published for the author by:
Orange Frazer Press
P.O. Box 214
Wilmington, OH 45177
Telephone: 937.382.3196 for price
and shipping information.
Website: www.orangefrazer.com

Book and cover design: Alyson Rua and Orange Frazer Press

Library of Congress Control Number: 2017957362

First Printing

*To my late wife, Donna.* I dedicate this book to her memory. She was the nicest person to ever walk this earth and I was so fortunate to have her as my wife. I certainly was playing at the "Broadway" level being married to her. She was an inspiration to me every day. She provided me with two children, a boy, Johnny, and a girl, Jackie, who carry forth her wonderful personality. I think one of the best things you can say about a person is that there was absolutely no one who didn't like her. I wish she was here to share my excitement in having published this book.

# Contents

# Preface

Paul Daugherty, who is a current outstanding sports writer for the *Cincinnati Enquirer* newspaper, wrote an article about me in *OHIO* magazine in January 1995, where he described me as "The World's Most Underrated Basketball Coach." I took that as a tremendous compliment. He remarked in the article that he had seen me mopping the gym floor on several occasions, which is certainly true.

In 1991, I did have a moment in the sun when I was asked to write an article on "Shot Discipline" for a book entitled *Coaching Basketball* which was edited by Jerry Krause. That book has articles by Adolph Rupp, Bobby Knight, John Thompson, Dean Smith, and John Wooden, just to name a few.

When I started to write this book, I looked for some comparison so that people reading the book could understand my experience; that they could understand the level at which I was coaching. The term of "Off-Broadway," according to its definition, matched exactly what I had experienced. Most organized basketball teams other than the elite Division I colleges and professional teams are Off-Broadway. The further down the food chain that you are coaching the more you will come under the definition. I am not trying to put down coaching at these levels. In fact, I think there should be a certain amount of pride in doing so, as they are the coaches who should be revered. Coaches at the Off-Broadway level can have as much impact or more, and it can be much more rewarding than the Broadway coach. According to my Theatre 101 book, written by Julie Halston, Off-Broadway is explained as:

Experimental
Imaginative
Small
Inexpensive
Away from the Broadway district
Far removed from
Non-commercial
Less publicized
A small theatre with less than 300 seats
Small scale

*Avant-garde—the advance group in any field, especially in the visual, literary, or musical arts, whose works are characterized chiefly by unorthodox, innovative, and experimental methods.

Of course Broadway is just the opposite. Halston explains in her book that, "Broadway is the center of the English-speaking theatre universe and is a dazzling piece of real estate called Manhattan. A play or musical earns the right to call itself 'Broadway' if it runs in one of the thirty-nine theatres that are considered Broadway houses." There are probably only about thirty-nine NCAA Division I basketball programs that have a chance to win a national championship, so those thirty-nine colleges are the Broadway programs. The designation is a crucial one, for only the shows in these theatres are eligible for the Tony Awards, the coveted prizes awarded each June to the new shows of the previous twelve months.

As an example, Broadway in the college basketball world is the NCAA Division I, sixty-eight colleges competing for a national championship each April at the Final Four. College basketball's version of getting a Tony Award. In reality, there may be only thirty-nine programs in college basketball that have a chance to win a national championship, if even that many. These teams are all 'Manhattan.'

The term Off-Broadway, I felt, explained my situation to the fullest. The schools where I coached were far away from NCAA Division I. Even Division II, or Division III and NAIA schools were light years away from the level that I was coaching. However, while at the University of Cincinnati Clermont, we were able to beat several of the NAIA and Division III schools we played, and we competed pretty well with some of the NCAA Division II schools. At the schools I coached, the crowds were small, the media interest was small, the budgets were small. We were basically non-profit and ticket prices were low, if they charged for the games at all. However, the quality of the play was good and very exciting. It was *basketball.*

While I coached at Ohio University, as a graduate assistant, I had the opportunity to work under two assistant coaches and a head coach who were outstanding. Jim Snyder, who was the head coach at Ohio University, had just beaten Kentucky and Michigan in the NCAA tournament. Dale Bandy was the number one assistant coach and later became the head coach at Ohio University. Bandy had one of the best basketball minds in the business. Mike

Schuler, who later became an NBA head coach at Portland and the LA Clippers, was the other assistant. Schuler was named the NBA Coach of the Year in 1987. Schuler had worked for Bobby Knight, so I had the opportunity to learn both the offensive and defensive systems of Mr. Knight. Bandy and Schuler became my gurus. I learned all I knew from these two men. Also, while I coached at Cincinnati State, I learned a lot from the gentleman that hired me, John Wagner. He taught me a lot about getting along with people and how to navigate the college atmosphere.

Coaching in what I call Off-Broadway, I had to come up with a system that would adapt to the ever-changing moons of the planet I was coaching on. I had to adjust to things like not having an assistant coach or limited practice time. However, this system had to be flexible, because things were constantly changing from the type of players each year to quality of opponents to other types of obstacles.

Except for those 300+ NCAA Division I teams, we are all coaching Off-Broadway to some extent. So I came up with ideas that worked at schools where there was less than what I needed to be a winner.

I had to be innovative in teaching the game, innovative in the offensive and defensive schemes, and innovative in my approach to the players. I had to adjust to the many obstacles that were presented. These ideas have been able to win 923 basketball games, so they have been somewhat successful ideas.

This book is intended for coaches and aspiring coaches at all levels, but particularly for the new coach. I am truly interested in writing this book to generate your thinking and to give you a

Coach John Hurley

Coach Hurley with 2006–2007 Men's Division II National Champs.

perspective on coaching Off-Broadway basketball. I want to pass on the things that worked for me. I became a head high school basketball coach my first year out of college. I knew very little about coaching the game, so I adopted a book called *Cincinnati Power Basketball,* written by the successful University of Cincinnati coach Ed Jucker. It became my bible and guide. I would have been lost if I hadn't had that book to refer too. I sincerely hope this book will become your bible or guide.

—*John Hurley*

# COACHING
# Off-Broadway Basketball

# 1 Statistical Help

One of the biggest problems at many of the Off-Broadway programs is being able to attain statistical help. Many programs don't keep game stats. It is very important to make sure you have that "Statistical Edge" and have someone do the game stats. It could be a parent, a volunteer, a student, a player on the bench, or anyone who has a little time to help. Even someone who doesn't know much about basketball can be trained to do them. Of course the Broadway programs have every basketball stat known to mankind available to them.

I also believe that statistics other than game stats need to be kept. OER and DER stats and a player efficiency chart are essential. They will be explained later in this chapter.

It is my belief that you need to have a statistical edge. If you are truly going to understand how your team is playing, and be able to make adjustments both with individual players or team strategy, you must have some statistical help.

It won't be long before the Broadway programs have even more statistical help. The current statistical systems in basketball give the coach some information, but not with the precision of baseball's sabermetrics. Statistical information, both offensive and defensive in basketball, is taking the next step. There is work being done out there to give the Broadway coach much more statistical information.

Rob Mahoney who is with SI.com believes that, "With next-level data collection in sight, we're now inching toward our metric future: a world of detailed, hyper-specific micro-statistics crafted to give us as much useful information as possible. Those statistics won't be perfect—numbers in basketball never are. But they'll finally offer the reliable quantitative component that offensive stats and especially defensive stats have never had, and it will foster a more complete comprehension of offensive and defensive play for coaches." But for the time being we will have to go with the statistical systems that we now have in place. Of course these statistical programs are just a pipe dream for the Off-Broadway coach.

## Offensive Efficiency Rating System (OER)

This is a possession evaluation system which can evaluate the effectiveness of your offense and defense. A team must have uninterrupted control of the basketball for it to be counted as a possession. The possession ends when the team no longer has complete control of the ball.

The easiest way to calculate total possessions is to count lost possessions. Most teams keep a shot chart which will give you shots attempted, shots made, foul shots attempted and made, and number of fouls. These statistics along with turnovers or loss of ball without a shot are the primary statistics that we need for possession evaluation.

## OER Chart (Used For Each Game)

| | |
|---|---|
| _____ shots for | _____ points |
| _____ times to foul line for | _____ points |
| _____ loss of ball | X |
| _____ total possessions for | _____ points |

Total points – total possessions =
Average points for each possessions =

Offense and Opponent Defense
Total Loss of Ball – Total Possessions =
Percent Loss of Ball

*Example:*

| | |
|---|---|
| 71 shots for | 74 points |
| 21 times to foul line for | 19 points |
| 14 loss of ball | X |
| 106 possessions for | 93 points |

93 – 106 = .88 points per possession
14 – 106 = 13% loss of ball

To calculate your team's DER you use the same statistics as shown of your opponent.

According to Dean Smith of North Carolina, who was one of the developers of this OER system, "Possession evaluation is determined by the average number of points scored for each possession of the ball by a team during the game. A perfect game from an offensive viewpoint would be an average of 2.00 points for each possession. The perfect defensive game would result in holding the opponent to 0.00 (scoreless). Our goals are to exceed .85 points per possession on offense and keep our opponents below .75 points per possession through our defensive efforts." Hopefully, I have explained this system well enough that you understand it, but you can get more information on this system on the internet.

## Player Efficiency Chart

The Player Efficiency Chart can be used to help players improve their play and it can also be used for the coach to get a better picture of how well his players are performing.

One of the things that I like about the Player Efficiency Chart is that the coach can take his philosophy on offense and defense and adjust it to his/her belief in the importance of each of the categories that the player is being evaluated. For example: If the coach's emphasis is on taking defensive charges he/she could change the points given for taking a charge.

The Player Efficiency Chart is a plus/minus system based on the coach's philosophy as to what he/she believes is important to the team's success.

*Example: Offensive Efficiency*

| | |
|---|---|
| 1. 2 pt. field goals attempted | -.75 |
| 2. 2 pt. field goals made | +2 |
| 3. 3 pt. field goals attempted | -1 |
| 4. 3 pt. field goals made | +3 |
| 5. Free throws attempted | -.75 |
| 6. Free throws made | +1 |
| 7. Offensive rebounds | +1.5 |
| 8. Assists | +1 |
| 9. Turnovers | -1 |

*Example: Defensive Efficiency*

| | |
|---|---|
| 1. 2 pt. baskets made by man you were guarding | -.5 points taken away for each 2 pts. given up |
| 2. 3 pt. baskets made by man you were guarding | -1 points taken away for each 3 pts. given up |
| 3. Defensive rebounds | +1 for each rebound |
| 4. Charges drawn | +2 each |
| 5. Deflections leading to a steal | +1 |
| 6. Deflections with no gain of possession | +.5 |
| 7. Steals | +1 |
| 8. Blocked shots | +1 |
| 9. Personal fouls | -1 |

This Player Efficiency Chart I have used for several years was developed by Dick Taylor of Clarion University. I have adjusted it and changed some of the components over the years. Understand that you can change the point totals to fit your philosophy.

John Hollinger, an ESPN statistician has developed a Player Efficiency Rating system for the NBA. In my understanding of this system, players are evaluated on an efficiency score for each minute that they play. You might want to Google this system to find out more about how the system is used.

It is my opinion that it is essential to use these types of statistical systems to help you coach. Basketball statistics can be misleading by themselves. For example, if your team scores 100 points, were you really efficient on offense, or was it just a fast-paced game? Or if you only give up 35 points on defense, did you really play well on defense, or did you or the other team hold the ball?

# 2 Get 'Em In Game Shape

Most of the Broadway programs have full-time strength coaches and athletic trainers to get their players in physical condition and to keep them in good physical condition. They also have *time* available prior to the season, during the season, and in the off-season to work on physical conditioning. The Off-Broadway coach does not have any of these opportunities. In youth basketball, there is very little time for conditioning. In junior high and high school many of the players may be coming off the football, soccer, or some other field. If you have any time at all, it may only be a few days. So, the Off-Broadway coach has to come up with other ideas to make sure their players are in somewhat decent condition.

Basketball is a very physically demanding game and the players must be in the best physical condition if they are going to be successful. It has been said by many that basketball is the most strenuous of all sports. The game calls for constant movement, numerous stops and starts, and instant changes in direction. Also, a lot of physical contact, jumping, sliding, and running at top speed is needed to play the game.

The philosophy that I have used is that we must find the time during the normal practice schedule to work on physical conditioning. But it must be explained to the players why you are doing the conditioning and for what reasons. They should not look upon what you are doing as punishment. These are the reasons I give them that we are doing extra conditioning in practice:

- Develops work ethic
- Raises your self-esteem
- Develops mental toughness
- Develops discipline
- Puts you in the proper frame of mind
- Develops poise and defensive stamina

My conditioning program consists of three different areas that are mandatory if your team is going to be in excellent condition to enhance your chance for individual and team success. The three areas are: 1. Run, Run and Run Some More 2. Weight Lifting or Weight Resistance 3. Nutrition.

## Run, Run, and Run Some More

In my estimation, running is the essence of any basketball conditioning program. As I mentioned, it is very important that your players don't relate running to being disciplined. It is important that they understand *why* you are running. I believe you can use running as a method of discipline, but the players must understand the goal of the running, even if it is for discipline.

In fact, I have always used the Peer Pressure Concept if a team or practice rule is violated, or if players are not practicing as hard as they should. This was a philosophy of Dean Smith at North Carolina University. If a rule is broken, we discipline as a team. I have always believed in group punishment for an individual violation. We have always played on the philosophy, "not to let your buddies down." The discipline usually consists of sprints or suicides, run by the entire team. So consequently, there are days that we get in a lot of running, which fulfills our Run, Run, and Run Some More concept. We also supplement our running in practice with several running drills, such as:

1. *Suicides*—This drill starts on the baseline and on the whistle the players sprint to the nearest foul line or foul line extended, then they sprint back and touch the baseline where they started, then they sprint to the half court line, and then sprint back to the end line, then they sprint to the far foul line or foul line extended, and then back to the baseline; and then lastly they sprint to the far baseline and sprint back to the baseline where they started. (I have used 30 seconds for timing this drill for all players. However, I have used 27 seconds for guards at times.)

2. *2-4-6-8 Figure Eight Drill*—We run three line figure eights starting with doing two (up and back counts one), then four, then six, and then eight. Each player runs the 2-4-6-8 figure eights. These are done using a ball and continuing until the designated number of figure eights is run. We shoot the lay-up at the end of each time up and down the floor. (If a lay-up is missed you do not count that figure eight.) We stress passing the ball up the floor and

going behind that man. The disadvantage of this drill is that it does take some time to complete.

3. *Chalk Drill*—Each player running the drill will draw with chalk, a circle on the near and far end line of the floor. The drill is run for one minute, and the player runs to the opposite end line, puts a chalk mark in the circle, runs back to the end line and makes another mark in the circle. This is done for one minute. Each day we strive for the player to get more marks in the circles. We usually have two players at a time run the drill.

4. *Cut Drill*—This drill is started in one of the corners of the gym. The player sprints to the near foul line elbow (elbow is where the vertical and horizontal lines come together of the foul circle) and touches the elbow, then sprints to half court elbow (where side line and half court line come together) and then sprints to far foul line elbow, and lastly to the corner elbow (where the side line comes together with the end line). We time this drill and try to improve every time we run it.

5. *Seventeens (17)*—The entire team spreads out on one of the side lines. On the whistle, the players sprint to the opposite side line and touch the line with their foot. This is a continuous drill run for time. The high school player must finish the 17 sprints in 70 seconds, girls should finish in 75 seconds, and college players should finish in 60 seconds. If all of the players don't make the time, then we run an eight (8) in half the time. We usually run this drill at the mid-point in practice, before we get a drink.

6. *Slingshots*—This drill is run like seventeens (17s), but it is more for short sprints. On the whistle the players run to the far foul line or foul line extended, then short sprint back to the opposite

foul line, then to the far end line, then back to the far foul line, and then short sprint to the opposite foul line, and then back to the end line where you started. We time this drill for each player.

The sport of basketball is specific in its methods of training. Basketball is an anaerobic sport, which means living in the absence of air or oxygen.

A lot of basketball coaches over the years have spent time having their players run long distances. Many coaches believed that their players should be on the cross-country team. However, this type of training may even hinder and impair recovery from the type of training needed for basketball. If your players do a lot of long, slow running, they will become efficient in that type of conditioning. This type of training is counter to the type of training that a basketball player needs. So instead of long, slow running, basketball requires a sprinting type of conditioning or training.

I have always taught my players that the work or effort needed in basketball is only for a short period of fifteen seconds per possession on defense. On offense it may be longer and a twenty to thirty second period of work or effort may be needed. Consequently, the type of conditioning needed is anaerobic endurance. There is a lot of stopping, starting, and changing directions in the game of basketball. There is also jumping and sprinting with short periods of rest or easy jogging or walking.

My pre-season conditioning program was built on the above ideas and philosophy. I put together what is called an interval training program. This program was developed keeping in mind that I was looking for that edge. I wanted our team to be in better shape than our opponents. The program was designed to have all drills at a high intensity level. I used a 3:1 work to rest ratio. The program was designed as follows:

*Interval Training Program*

1. Short sprints for 15–90 seconds.

2. Work outs no more than 30–45 minutes.

3. Repeat drills 5–15 times.

4. Always used time, perimeter players 27 seconds and post 30 seconds for suicides.

5. Used 60 seconds for rest.

You may also want to include a few minutes of aerobic exercise, but I wouldn't use any more than 20% of your work out time. You can do some distance running up to a mile. I would only use aerobic training as a supplement to your anaerobic training program.

## Weight Lifting or Weight Resistance

According to nationally known personal trainer Claude Parcon, who works with athletes of all ages, children can start lifting weights around puberty, or thirteen-fourteen years of age. He states that, "he has trained kids from ages nine–twelve in simple strength training like resistance bands, light free weights, and body weight exercises. Ages fifteen–sixteen is where they will experience the more traditional set of exercises like bench press and overhead squats. Keep the weight light with high reps. Don't take the chance of damaging growth plates by lifting too heavy."

The American Academy of Pediatrics, the American College of Sports Medicine, and the National Strength and Conditioning Association, all support strength training for kids. But only if done using proper technique, safety, and monitored at all times.

In a study done at the Mayo Clinic, even children as young as seven or eight years old can start some sort of strength program, consisting of only one's own body resistance.

Bill Foran and Robin Pound in their book, *Complete Conditioning For Basketball,* emphasize a bench press program. Their program consists of the following:

| *"Bench Press* | *Lift* | *Warm Up—5 reps* |
|---|---|---|
| NBA and Male College | 185 lbs. | 135 lbs. |
| Male – High School | 135 lbs. | 95 lbs. |
| WNBA and Female College | 95 lbs. | 65 lbs. |
| Female – High School | 75 lbs. | 45 lbs. |

Do 10 push ups first and rest for 60 seconds. Then warm-up, rest 90 seconds, then lift. Do as many reps as you can do—maximum number of reps."

I believe in weight lifting or training for basketball players. It is important to get a trainer to design a program for your players. Usually there is a program for off-season weight lifting and in-season weight lifting. Make sure you know what you are doing before implementing any kind of weight program.

# Nutrition

For most Off-Broadway coaches, nutrition is the most difficult situation to control. The Broadway Division I programs all have training tables. It is pretty easy for them to have their players eating the proper foods. However, the small college coaches, high school coaches, and below don't have that privilege. So the Off-Broadway coach needs to know as much about nutrition for basketball players as he or she can learn. The following article is by Paul Frabritz, founder of PJF Performance (Tempe, Arizona) and top performance enhancement coach and was originally published on STACK.com. It contains the latest nutrition information for basketball players:

"Many experts believe that the difference between becoming a good player and a great player is your diet. The proof is in the physiques and performance of today's top NBA stars. These athletes stay under 10% body fat and have both a solid diet and weightlifting plan. There is a trend in the way these athletes eat as they all share the following five superior dietary habits:

1. *They Eat Protein at Every Meal*—Protein is the most important macronutrient you can eat when trying to achieve a lean physique. It builds muscle while increasing your metabolism so you can continually burn fat. You are not eating a real meal if your plate doesn't have at least 20 grams of protein.

Aim to eat 0.75 to 1 gram of protein per pound of body weight.

The majority of your intake should be from real protein sources (e.g., chicken, fish, grass-fed beef, eggs, turkey, quinoa, Greek yogurt and mixed nuts).

Within 30 minutes after a workout, drink a protein shake or chocolate milk in order to quickly provide a flow of amino acids to your muscles.

2. *They Tailor Carbohydrate Intake to Daily Workout Demands*—Every day you should consume a high level of protein and healthy fats. But your carbohydrate intake should change with your day's activity. On light off days you will need fewer carbohydrates.

Stay away from simple carbohydrates throughout the day (e.g., candy, sugary drinks and white bread). Stick to complex carbohydrates (e.g., oatmeal, sweet potatoes, fruits, vegetables, and legumes).

45 to 90 minutes prior to a demanding workout, consume a small amount of complex, slow digesting carbohydrates.

After hard workouts, consume at least a 2:1 ratio of carbohydrates to protein. Generally this will be around 40 grams of carbs and 20 grams of protein.

Lean toward simple, fast-digesting carbs immediately after workouts to spike insulin and increase anabolism.

After light workouts, consume 1:1 ratio of carbs to protein.

3. *They Don't Rely on Supplements*—To get lean, you need to eat real, nutrient-dense foods. The base of your diet should never be supplements. That is a costly mistake. If your diet is broken, no amount of supplementation will fix it.

Use protein powder only in your post-workout shakes.

Three essential supplements belong in your kitchen: fish oil, vitamin D and protein powder.

You may take a multivitamin to ensure you don't have any vitamin and mineral deficiencies.

4. *They Eat Breakfast Every Day*—Lean athletes eat breakfast every day. Numerous studies show that eating a high protein breakfast helps maintain a lower body fat percentage.

Eat at least 20 grams of protein for breakfast.

Stay away from sugary cereals.

Consume a combination of protein, carbohydrates and fat.

Hydrate well during breakfast.

5. *They Develop Food Preparation Strategies* People turn to fast food because they don't have time to prepare high-quality meals throughout the day.

Spend time in the kitchen preparing meals.

Pack plastic bags full of almonds or trail mix for snacks.

If you have trouble waking up early enough to cook breakfast, cook hard-boiled eggs for an instant high protein breakfast.

Go grocery shopping every three days."

As I will be mentioning several times in this book, the Off Broadway coach needs an edge. Having your team in top physical condition is a must, and it can be done during normal practice if needed. The information that I have provided above is what has worked for me over the years. I believe it's important to be an expert in conditioning (running), weight training, and nutrition. It's like Clint Eastwood in his movie "The Outlaw Josey Wales." He needed an edge and it was always having his back to the sun before he pulled his guns.

# 3 The Science of Shot Discipline

"The Science of Shot Discipline" is an area that in my opinion has no deferential. It is the same at the Broadway level as it is at the Off-Broadway level. And I think that we can actually learn some things from what is going on at the Broadway level in terms of shot discipline. No matter what level you are coaching basketball, it is a must to teach shot discipline to your players.

Shot discipline should be one of the first things that the young basketball player should be taught. As you read this chapter, keep in mind that a basketball player at any level must feel comfortable and free to shoot the basketball. However, if he or she learns shot discipline and has an understanding of it, your player and your team will be much more proficient.

If you look closely at the NCAA Statistics Services 21-year study of Division I basketball trends, the answer to the above question is beginning to take shape. So, for the young coach looking to decide what he/she is going to teach concerning shot discipline, the following statistics might help you make that determination:

1. In 1994, NCAA Division I Men's Basketball Teams took an average of 60.6 shots per game. In 2015, Division I Men's Basket-

ball Teams took an average of 54.24 shots per game. This is a difference of 6.36 shots per game, and the number of shots seemed to decline each year. Is this a clue that teams are being more concerned with shot discipline?

2. In a two year span, field-goal percentage is down. During 2014, teams shot at a 44.24% percent rate. In 2015, teams shot at a 43.49% percent rate, a difference of .75%. Even though this is not a huge difference, shooting percentage was down. Is this a clue that coaches have pulled off the reins on shooting?

3. The percentage of three-point shots attempted during this 21-year period of time shows an increase in number of three-point attempts. In 2010, an average of 6.25 attempts was made. In 2015, an average of 6.41 attempts was made. A difference of .16 attempts is another clue that coaches have emphasized taking better shots.

4. This last statistic may provide the most evidence that coaches are teaching shot discipline. In 1994, teams averaged 75.00 points per game. In 2015, teams averaged 67.74 points per game which is a difference of 7.26 points per game. That difference seems to be significant. There are probably several factors responsible for this difference in scoring, such as better defense, rule changes, etc., but I believe coaches teaching shot discipline has to be one of the factors.

These statistics indicate to me that the science of shot discipline is certainly not dead. Fewer shots being taken and fewer points being scored indicates that something is going on. I think the fact that players can be enamored with the three-point shot and the importance of the three-point shot in winning, does show maybe a loosening of the shooting reins by coaches. Shooting percentage is down a little which could also indicate a loosening of the reins by coaches. However, I believe the fact that teams are taking fewer shots (6.36 shots per game) indicate to me that shot discipline is being taught.

If my analysis of these statistics is correct, then Division I Men's coaches are still teaching shot discipline, but there is probably a tendency to play a little more up-tempo with more emphasis on the three-point shot.

As always, the Division I coaches usually have great influences on the style of play at all levels. With all the talk about run-and-gun basketball in 1994, I was really starting to question some of my philosophies on shot discipline. It was very reassuring to me after looking at the statistics that even though there may be something of a trend toward this open style of play there is enough evidence to show that shot discipline is still being taught, and, of course, shot discipline can actually be taught in a run-and-shoot system. However, the principles are more suited to a little slower pace. With all this in mind I would like to offer the following ideas on shot discipline.

## Philosophies Involved In Shot Discipline

In order to be successful in teaching players shot discipline, coaches must understand the philosophy behind the science. They must be able to explain to players why shot discipline is important to success.

The ideas that support this philosophy of shot discipline are as follows:

1. While it is true that many players are excellent shooters from the outside, our belief is that any player can be a good shooter in the high-percentage area close to the basket.

2. Playing basketball is not an equal-opportunity game. Some players must be passers, others rebounders, and few shooters.

3. Winning and losing come down to a matter of the number of times your team has possession of the basketball, and how effective you are in scoring when you do have possession.

4. The score and amount of time left to play is very important to the science of shot discipline.

5. Realization that the three-point shot is a tremendous weapon, but must not be abused.

## Definition of a Good Shot

My definition of a good shot has been structured by my philosophies of shot discipline. Your players must have a clear understanding of what your definition of a good shot means. You must be careful that your players don't perceive your definition of a good shot as simply not shooting. Characteristics of a good shot are:

1. Unguarded (no defensive pressure)
2. In range (length of shot)
3. Balanced (head in the center of the body)

The easiest method to determine shot discipline is to test the players in practice. I like to test our players in the following manner:

1. All players are tested at 15 feet and the 3 point line.

2. They must make 65% on the 15 foot shot and 50% of the 3 point shot, shooting unguarded. If they can't, they may not take those shots in practice or a game.

3. Each player must prove to the coach that he can shoot the proper percentage in practice.

*Using shot charts is very important to determining shot selection. Basically, coaches should chart every shot taken in practice and games. However, with youth teams this may not be realistic, because there are not enough coaches or staff to carry this out.

## The Magnificent Twelve of Shot Discipline

1. Keep in mind that drawing the foul and stepping to the free throw line is a high-percentage shot.

2. Remember that outside shots are always available.

3. Get the ball inside whenever possible.

4. Knowing when not to shoot is as important as knowing when to shoot.

5. Make the extra pass. Shoot only when you know there is not a teammate open in a higher percentage area.

6. Shoot only when you know you have a good team rebounding advantage.

7. Poor shot selection can result in a loss.

8. Remember that mental and physiological factors can affect shooting.

9. Study tape and point out to players what is a good or bad shot.

10. Taking good shots does not necessarily mean you will score fewer points.

11. If a player is taking bad shots, a reprimand of some type should come from the coach. (It's best to do this early in the season)

12. It's not "your" shot, it is "our" shot. There is no such thing as "my" shot.

In conclusion, let me emphasize three very important points on shot discipline:

1. Whatever your offensive scheme, allow yourself the greatest mathematical chance of succeeding by coaching your team on shot discipline.

2. Develop your offense through shot discipline concepts to allow your team to have more efficiency per offensive possession.

3. Remember the word discipline means training, regimen, drill, practice, obedience, restraint, control, punishment, and correction.

In my opinion, it is essential to teach shot discipline to your players no matter what level you are coaching. In order to give yourself the greatest chance of winning, shot discipline must be understood by your players.

* See NCAA Statistics Services 6-Year Study of Division I Trends on page 187.

# 4 Teaching Shooting

One of the things that I never learned much about in my early years in coaching was how to teach my players to shoot the basketball. But I had the opportunity to be around what I think were the best teachers of shooting fundamentals that I have ever known when I started working with a shoe company by the name of Pro-Keds in the late 1970s. Pro-Keds had two men on their staff who conducted clinics on shooting. They were George Lehmann and Lavaughn Robertson. They were both outstanding teachers and they had broken the shot down piece by piece. Of course Pro-Keds does not make basketball shoes any longer, but I will never forget everything I learned from their shooting clinics.

It is my belief that shooters are not born—they are made. I believe that if a player is willing to dedicate himself or herself to getting better at shooting the basketball that it can be done. I have seen many examples of improvement in shooting over the years and I think Lebron James is a good example. I believe that during his first couple of years in the NBA he made great strides in improving his shooting. I think that Michael Jordan improved as well.

Improvement in shooting is all about repetition and muscle memory. The more you shoot the better you will be.

The first time that I heard the terminology for teaching shooting was in 1979. I had never heard the four basic fundamentals of shooting, which was consolidated down to simply: B-E-E-F (each letter in the word represents an important fundamental). Lehmann and Robertson told the players, just think of the word: B-E-E-F. Without a doubt it all starts with the term B-E-E-F.

Here is a breakdown of the word B-E-E-F as it relates to shooting the basketball.

## Balance

*Coaching Points:*

1. Legs must always be on balance.

2. Head must be kept still and in the center of your body.

3. Put one foot in front of the other—shooting/lead foot forward and "toe to the target."

4. Legs as wide as shoulders.

5. Use legs for power—bend the knees to be in triple threat position (dribble-pass-shoot).

In my estimation, keeping your head still is the most important part of balance. This is as true with free throws as it is with perimeter shots.

## Eyes On The Target

*Coaching Points:*

1. Eyes must be focused on the basket.
2. Shoot for the front center of the rim.
3. Do not follow the flight of the ball with your eyes.
4. There must be concentration at all times.
5. In your mind, block out everything but the basket.

A real problem with younger players is that they have a tendency to follow the path of the basketball when they shoot.

## Elbow Keeps The Basketball Straight

*Coaching Points:*

1. The elbow should be under the ball and straight. (Do not allow your shooting elbow to stick out to the side or be on an angle.)

2. When the elbow is straight and under the ball, the shooting hand will automatically be placed on the ball correctly.

3. Have your elbow over your shooting foot. (Right foot for right handers and left foot for left handers.)

## Follow Through

*Coaching Points:*

1. Every time you shoot the ball, follow through.

2. Try to stick your shooting hand right in the basket (stick your hand in the cookie jar).

3. Make sure you have a full arm extension.

4. Guide hand should be on side of ball only shooting hand follows-through.

5. Don't snap your shooting hand back.

6. Make your follow through smooth and consistent.

## Drill To Teach BEEF

You should have the player stand in front of the basket, balanced, and about a couple of steps from the front of the rim. The player should hold the ball out in front with their palm up to the sky. Then the player brings the ball into shooting position (shooting hand only) with their elbow straight and eyes on the basket. The player bends their knees and shoots the ball with one hand, trying not to hit the rim. Then follow through after the release of the ball.

## R-O-B-O-T

R-O-B-O-T (Range, Open, Balance, One-Count, Teammates) is another shooting fundamental acronym that connects with the fundamentals of B-E-E-F. I have used a combination of the two ideas to teach the fundamentals of shooting. The R-O-B-O-T explanation goes along with my ideas of shot selection.

### Range

*Coaching Points:*

1. Only shoot when you are in your range.

2. Some players have longer shooting ranges than others.

3. If you cannot shoot 60% in shooting practice from a particular area of the floor with no defense, then you shouldn't be shooting from that range.

### Open

*Coaching Points:*

1. A player should not shoot when he or she is not open (unguarded).

2. If you are not open when you get the ball, get the ball to someone who is.

## Balance

*Coaching Points:*

1. This is one of the BEEF's fundamentals as well. (This emphasizes the importance of this fundamental that it is covered twice.)

2. As was stated earlier, the head is the most important factor in balance.

## One-Count

*Coaching Points:*

1. The shot should be one-count from start to finish.

2. Step into the pass with hands in the ready position and quickly shoot the basketball.

3. Do not dip the basketball before the shot.

4. Shots should not be attempted off a bad pass.

5. The shot should be smooth and with a consistent shooting motion.

## Teammates

*Coaching Points:*

1. If a teammate has a better shot, pass the ball to them.

2. Shooting without passing the ball to your teammates is not usually advised.

*I have always believed that the coach should video tape a player's shot. It is important to let the player see what mistakes, if any, there are to his or her shot. It is a great way to emphasize the shooting fundamentals.

## Two Types Of Shots

1. *Set shot*—Usually younger players. (Player sights over the ball.)

2. *Jump shot*—Usually older players. (Player sights under the ball.)

*B-E-E-F can be taught with both shots.

## Triple Threat Position

Before teaching the shooting fundamentals, it is important to teach the triple threat position. As I have mentioned earlier, the triple threat position must be accomplished before the shot attempt. The position must be secured, so that a player can either shoot, pass, or dribble. All of the fundamentals of balance must come into effect.

## Other Coaching Points

1. A coach does not have to be a good shooter to be a great teacher of shooting.

2. Feet, hips, and shoulders should be square to the basket.

3. The palm should not touch the ball on the grip of the shooting hand.

4. There are four ways to miss a shot. Right, left, short, or long. Player should only miss short or long if their elbow is straight.

5. On long shot player must use their legs.

6. Extend the elbow above the eyebrow on follow through.

7. Freeze the follow through—hold the follow through until the ball goes through the basket.

8. The thumbs should form a "T" when gripping the ball for the shot.

9. It is important to cock your wrist when you bring the ball in position to shoot.

10. It is important for players to always step into the shoot when receiving a pass.

11. It is important for players to square up on the inside foot when shooting off a screen or off the dribble.

12. The shooting fundamentals BEEF are also very important in shooting free throws.

## The Jump Shot

I believe it is important to single out the jump shot in discussing the fundamentals of shooting. The fundamentals of shooting the jump shot are the same, as in BEEF. George Lehmann explained the jump shot as follows; "right foot is always in front of my left. When I land after my jump shot, I am always on balance and ready to play, I do not follow my shot. Fading away during the jump shot is probably the worst habit a jump shooter can create. The best habit is to go straight up and down. If you must move, move towards the target. This will keep your rhythm and help maintain concentration."

Side note: All of George Lehmann's instructional shooting clinics are on YouTube.

## Foul Shooting Fundamentals

Again, the B-E-E-F fundamentals are used when shooting from the foul line. Actually, the fundamentals may be even more important when shooting a free throw.

*Coaching Points:*

1. Player's should have a pre-shot routine. (Take a deep breath.)

2. Physical fundamentals—B-E-E-F will make for a perfect free throw.

3. Mental fundamentals—Concentration is the key word. I tell players to concentrate on three things: (1) keeping their head still, (2) following through, and (3) staying on the free throw line, not backing off the line when they shoot.

4. Record makes and misses in practice, give a prize for the weekly winner.

## Record Every Shot

This is one idea that I have always thought was very important when practicing shooting. I think the player trying to improve his or her shot should record every shot. I believe it is important to know how many shots you make or miss when practicing shooting. I tell players to make a chart and record makes and misses from the different spots on the basketball floor.

There is even a new electronic device that can help players track their shot attempts with makes and misses. This device is called a ShotTracker. It is a simple device that you put on the net that records on an app on your phone. If interested contact, www.shottracker.com.

According to the website mytowntutors.com and this article, "Coaching Youth Basketball: BEEF = Good Shooting Form," "for a coach to be successful at teaching players how to shoot the basketball correctly, there needs to be a complete understanding of the fundamental of a shot (BEEF). A coach does not have to be a great shooter or even a fair shooter to be a great teacher of shooting. The coach simply must understand BEEF and be able to explain the fundamentals to the players. The coach also needs to have knowledge of a teaching progression and age-appropriate drills that will help players develop the proper shooting fundamentals."

# 5 Pre-Season Tryout Plan

Choosing your team comes with the territory of being a basketball coach. Even the Broadway coach has to offer a scholarship to a selected few. Some players that were hoping for that scholarship get left out. There's no way around it, it's part of the coach's job, but how we handle it is what is important. There must be a plan.

When I was coaching high school and college basketball, there was nothing I dreaded more than cutting players. I was cut a couple times trying out for teams and I know what an emotional impact it can have on some kids. I always looked for ways to keep as many players as possible. When I was coaching in college I usually didn't cut players, but just let them cut themselves as the season went on.

I think it is very important for a coach at any level to have a plan for pre-season tryouts. Planning is very important to make sure that you have a strategy for choosing your team and to be organized to the point that nothing is overlooked. Of course as mentioned, whether you like it or not, cutting the team is part of the role of being a head basketball coach.

Let's first look at the positive side of the whole situation on tryouts and having to select the team. Sometimes when a player gets cut, it is the most important situation in moving a person toward where they should actually be.

"I've got a book by Harvey MacKay called *We Got Fired: And It's the Best Thing That Ever Happened to Us*," says Dr. Tom Hanson of webball.com. He goes on to say that, "The book is loaded with chapter after chapter of well-known people such as Joe Torre, Lou Holtz, Bill Belichick, Muhammad Ali, Jesse Ventura and many business people like Donald Trump and Larry King who were bummed out when they got canned."

I played basketball in the seventh and eighth grade, but was cut my freshmen year. I had pretty good skills but I was very thin and I just didn't have the strength I needed. Getting cut gave me time to condition and get stronger and I eventually made the high school team.

Even though I didn't like getting cut, it gave me the motivation to continue trying to make the team. So sometimes it can work out but other times the best thing for the player is to move on to something else.

"You're snuffing out a kid's dream. If it doesn't hurt, you're either a jerk or so evolved that you don't see how much you are hurting him/her," said Dr. Tom Hanson, webball.com.

I developed five rules or procedures to help me with the task of cutting the team. I do believe that these rules made it a little easier, if there is such a thing. The rules are:

1. *Give Players a Preview*

You must explain to the players that everyone is not going to make the team and that they should try as hard as possible so there will be no regrets. Tell them if they didn't make the team this year, if they work really hard, they could make the team next year. I like to leave it open ended and positive if possible.

2. *Give Evaluation—Why They Got Cut*

I think it is very important to give the player and the parents an evaluation as to why the player didn't make the team. This could be a written evaluation or you could set up a meeting with the player and parents. Always include the areas that the player needs to work on so they have a chance to make the team next year.

3. *Cutting Should Be The Last Option*

Especially with younger players, don't cut unless you absolutely have to. Figure out a way to keep all of the players who tried out. You may have to be creative, but make every consideration.

4. *Have A Point Evaluation System*

The coach should decide on several criteria (3-5) and a point value (1–10) should be given to each one. Areas that you might evaluate are: (1) skills, (2) athletic ability, (3) attitude, and (4) coachability. Devise a chart that you can use for your evaluation of each player.

5. *Have A Tryout Practice Plan*

I believe that it is imperative to have a practice plan that allows the players trying out to show their basketball fundamentals and also their game skills. Drills and scrimmaging both need to be done.

"Be careful to judge young big's, especially, because some need time and some develop late." —Rick Pitino.

Here is a sample tryout practice plan that I like to use:

## Tryout Practice Plan

*5 Minutes:* Stretching.

*5 Minutes:* Lay-Ups.

*5 Minutes:* Three Person Weave.

*7 Minutes:* 3 Line Dribbling (sideline to sideline).

1. Speed Dribble (up with the right hand back with the left).
2. Cross-Over (zig zag ball up the floor crossing over with each change of direction).
3. Spin Move (going right then left up the floor and back).
4. Behind the back (zig zag the ball up the floor).

*3 Minutes:* Person-In-The-Middle Drill—Two players space themselves twelve feet apart facing each other, one has a basketball. Put a defensive player in the middle. The middle person runs and puts pressure on the person with the ball and the person with the ball tries to pass around the defense by using ball fakes. The drill continues until the middle person touches the ball, then that player takes the middle. No dribbling and use the pivot foot.

*5 Minutes:* Low Post Drop Step Lay-Ups— Have players catch the ball drop step, take a power dribble and finish the lay-up.

*5 Minutes:* Foul Shooting—Teach BEEF shooting fundamentals. Balance-Eyes on target-Elbow straight-Follow through.

*5 Minutes:* Defensive Slides—Stance and slide right and left.

*10 Minutes:* 3-on-3—Play to 3 points and rotate teams.

*15 Minutes:* 5-on-5—Full court, play to 5 points and rotate teams.

*This practice plan would take 65 minutes, but add in time for water breaks.

## Make Known Your Cuts

Without any doubt, making your cuts known is the most difficult part of the whole tryout. Here are some methods that have been used by coaches to make cutting easier.

1. Gather the team around and verbally tell each player who was cut why they were cut. Thank them for coming out and tell them to work hard and try again next year.
2. Put up a list with players who made the team. Those not on the list were cut.
3. Meet privately with each cut player to discuss his strengths and weaknesses.
4. Give each player who tried out an envelope and tell them not to open it until they have left the gym.

## Miscellaneous Ideas For Tryouts

Opinions vary on the ideal number of players for a team, but most coaches believe that 12 to 15 is the right number.

Always look out for the potential of the player.

Always have the evaluation sheet available for players and parents to see, or set up a meeting to discuss the evaluation sheet. Rank the players.

Make sure you get as many coaches at the tryouts to help evaluate the players. The more feedback the better.

Try to mix the tryout teams with equal talent as much as possible.

Document the how and why of selected players and those who were cut.

One of the most important factors to consider when choosing a team is positional skill set.

Face the issue of cutting the team head on.

Don't lie or "sugarcoat" why any player was cut.

Don't give false encouragement.

Never compare players.

Don't use the term "cut from the team." Tell them "they didn't make the team this year."

"Ultimately, the best way to cut a player is with your heart." —Dr. Tom Hanson

At the end of this chapter, I have put in a sample Player Evaluation Form that you may want to consider using when selecting your teams.

# Basketball Tryout Evaluation Form

Player's Name: ______________________________ Age: ________

Position: ____________________________________________

Height: ______________ Weight: ______________ Grade: ______________

Experience: __________________________________________

## SKILLS

| | | | | *Summary* |
|---|---|---|---|---|
| *Shooting:* | | | | |
| *Field Goals* | Poor | Adequate | Excellent | ______________ |
| *Foul Shots* | Poor | Adequate | Excellent | ______________ |
| | | | | ______________ |
| *Dribbling:* | | | | ______________ |
| *Right Hand* | Poor | Adequate | Excellent | ______________ |
| *Left Hand* | Poor | Adequate | Excellent | ______________ |
| | | | | ______________ |
| *Passing:* | | | | ______________ |
| *Perimeter* | Poor | Adequate | Excellent | ______________ |
| *Into Post* | Poor | Adequate | Excellent | ______________ |
| | | | | ______________ |
| *Rebounding:* | | | | ______________ |
| *Boxing Out* | Poor | Adequate | Excellent | ______________ |
| *Hunts Ball* | Poor | Adequate | Excellent | ______________ |

*Offensive Moves:*

| | | | |
|---|---|---|---|
| *Perimeter* | Poor | Adequate | Excellent |
| *Post* | Poor | Adequate | Excellent |

*Defense:*

| | | | |
|---|---|---|---|
| *Individual* | Poor | Adequate | Excellent |
| *Team* | Poor | Adequate | Excellent |

*Athletic Ability:*

| | | | |
|---|---|---|---|
| *Speed* | Poor | Adequate | Excellent |
| *Quickness* | Poor | Adequate | Excellent |

*Coachability:*

| | | | |
|---|---|---|---|
| *Attitude* | Poor | Adequate | Excellent |
| *Listens* | Poor | Adequate | Excellent |

*Team:*

| | | | |
|---|---|---|---|
| *Unselfish* | Poor | Adequate | Excellent |
| *Leadership* | Poor | Adequate | Excellent |

______________________________

______________________________

______________________________

______________________________

Strengths:______________________

______________________________

______________________________

______________________________

______________________________

Weaknesses:_____________________

______________________________

______________________________

______________________________

______________________________

Overall Rating: 5 4 3 2 1

______________________________

______________________________

Evaluator:_______________________

Date:___________________________

Player Evaluation Form Prepared by John Hurley

# 6 Develop Your Philosophy and What You Want to Emphasize

The first thing you should do the minute you find out you are going to be coaching basketball is to develop your philosophy. This philosophy can always be changed or adjusted, but you must have one so that you have a direction to follow. It is likely that you still might be determining your philosophy, but get something down on paper. We will take a look at some ideas on putting a philosophy together and also having a guide that can help you develop this philosophy. Most Broadway coaches are pretty good about developing their philosophies but they have a much more consistent situation in terms of the type of players they coach and the competition they are playing against than the Off-Broadway coach.

Not only do you need to develop your philosophy, but you need to determine what you are going to emphasize and it must list the priorities. For example: defense might be your first priority and rebounding might be your second. I will give you a plan and some ideas on how to develop these priorities in this chapter.

## Guideline For Developing A Philosophy

I think the best definition of a *coaching philosophy* that I have seen is by Pat Anderson: "Simply put, it's a set of beliefs that define the priorities and values of the coach."

The following guide can help you put your philosophy together. You can add or delete any of these suggestions, but it will give you some framework as to what you might consider in your philosophy:

1. Teamwork
2. Positive attitude
3. Work ethic/effort
4. Handling adversity
5. Defense
6. Ideas on discipline
7. Tempo (slow or fast)
8. Rebounding
9. Offense (free lance or set plays)
10. Defining players' roles
11. Winning and losing
12. Developing character
13. Building confidence
14. Setting goals
15. Style of play

I believe that there is one issue that probably needs to be identified when you are putting your philosophy together and that is the amount of talent you have on the team. This might determine how you can play. What this comes down to sometimes, as I have discussed before in this book, is the *System Versus Flexible Approach.* The *system-type* coach will make adjustments based on his/her talent on the team; whereas, the *flexible-type* coach will change the system from year to year, based on the talent.

Your personality has a lot to do with developing your philosophy. For example: if you are an aggressive person, you might want to play an aggressive style of defense and offense. Playing a more passive style of defense and offense might conflict with your personality.

Also, I believe that the formation of your philosophy will definitely be influenced by the experiences you have had, both in playing basketball and in observing the game.

Usually the best advice is to be yourself and don't try to copy what some other coach is doing. However, I don't see anything wrong with getting ideas of other coaches and evaluating them as to how they would fit into your philosophy.

"How do you go from where you are to where you want to be? I think you have to have an enthusiasm for life. You have to have a dream, a goal and you have to be willing to work for it."
—Jim Valvano

## Set Your Priorities And Points of Emphasis

Setting your priorities and figuring out what to emphasize is as important as developing your philosophy. For me this was always difficult because I wanted to put everything down as my priority. I had trouble zeroing in on a few important points and always put in too many points of emphasis. You need to develop a few points in your mind that are superior and stick with them. According to Jeff Haefner of www.basketballbreakthrough.com, "In the business world, we use a similar concept. We often talk about 'Focusing On The Critical Few,' versus the, 'Trivial Many.'" This is a good concept to remember.

Morgan Wootten, the outstanding high school basketball coach, has set the following priorities for his team:

1. God
2. Family
3. School
4. Basketball

I had three priorities for my teams that I would repeat to them before we took the floor before every game:

1. Play hard
2. Play smart
3. Play together

Here are some other priorities or points of emphasis that you might consider:

1. Attitude
2. Put kids first
3. Individual development
4. Teach life skills
5. Accept responsibility
6. Outstanding communication
7. Highly organized
8. First class style

9. Commitment to the program

10. Academics first

Here are a couple of secondary core beliefs that I used that I think are very important:

1. *Belief in a player's potential.*

I never gave up on a kid, I always believed that he/she was going to get better. I even recruited many players who I saw potential in, but were not ready to play at that moment.

2. *Honesty*

I was for the most part brutally honest with my players. I learned that they respected that.

3. *Fairness*

I tried to treat all the players the same.

4. *Staying connected to your players over time.*

I tried to do this as much as possible. I still befriend many of my players on Facebook and by telephone.

"Create unselfishness as the most important team attribute." —Bill Russell

Of course it is one thing to develop your priorities, but the biggest task at hand is to get your players to buy in to them.

According to Pat Riley in his book *The Winner Within*, as a player you are either *in* or you are *out,* there is no in-between. There has to be a team commitment to your philosophy and to your priorities, and everyone has to be on board. This has to be addressed quite often with your team, as players may go back and forth on their acceptance of your philosophy and priorities.

# 7 Practice

How you deal with practice as a coach is what separates the men from the boys, or shall I say the Broadway coaches from the Off-Broadway coaches. I have known Broadway coaches who came to practice with their practice plan hand written on a napkin. And I have known Off-Broadway coaches who have come to practice with the most detailed practice plan, which was planned to the very second, and left nothing to chance. This is an area where there are no obstacles for the Off-Broadway coach. He has the same time as the Broadway coach, 24 hours per day!

I cannot emphasize enough the importance of practice. Basketball practice should be treated like the most difficult academic class your players have. The gym should be considered the coaches classroom and the coach must be the teacher.

There are many things in coaching basketball that could be considered the most important; however I don't believe you would get much of an argument from most outstanding basketball coaches that practice and planning practice are the most important things they do in coaching basketball.

"Practice is sacred." —Fran Fraschilla

Basketball practice sessions should be split into two areas:

1. Individual development
2. Team development

It's very important to save time in practice for individual instruction and working on fundamentals. This will produce the greatest improvement in your players. Coach Wootten believed that, "the teaching of fundamentals, until they are executed quickly, properly, and without conscious thought, is prerequisite to playing the game."

One of the things I learned at Ohio University is to take every opportunity to work with the players individually. Of course we had probably five coaches and two managers on the practice floor at one time to work with players. We would take any period of down time in practice to sneak in a few minutes working individually with players. We also used time before practice and after practice to work individually with players.

You must also work on the team aspects of the game. But don't overlook the time you need to spend on the fundamentals and player improvement, because you want to put in some kind of magical offense. I have seen coaches spend most of their practice time working on plays or some kind of exotic offense. You must develop the fundamentals first.

My high school coach, George Heller, understood this concept very well. At least 75% of his practice was devoted to working on dribbling drills, passing drills, footwork drills, shooting drills, fast break drills, etc. Coach Heller won a couple Ohio State Basketball Championships, so his idea seems to work.

For coaches who are coaching young players under the high school level, I believe it is important to adhere to these philosophies:

1. Teaching kids fundamentals is much more important than winning games.

2. Spending more time on fundamentals will actually help you win more games.

The biggest frustration for me as a basketball coach was finding enough time to practice. In pre-season, I always wanted to have at least two and a half to three hours for practice. Usually I was lucky to get an hour and a half. I know a lot of you may only have an hour or maybe only an hour per week. So it becomes very important to do a good job planning practice in order to get the most out of it. "Don't sacrifice fundamentals because of time limitations!"

I tried to follow a practice time schedule during the season. Practice time was not always available to my liking, but I tried to do the following:

1. Beginning of season—2+ hours of practice
2. After Christmas—1½ hours of practice
3. Tournament time—1 hour to 1 hour 15 minutes of practice

In order to get the most time I could for practice, I would do things such as bring the players in before school to shoot free throws or work on shooting. One of the things I eventually did because of limited practice time was use pre-game warm-ups as a mini-practice. Usually you are given at least 20 minutes for warm-ups before games. Sometimes if you are playing the first game, you can get onto the floor sooner and get even more time. Basically, during pregame warm up sessions I worked on the following areas:

*Mini Pre-game Practice Session*

4 on 4 defensive shell—The ball is moved, help side, ball pressure, stop penetration.

1 on 1 in post— The rest of team does defensive zig zags.

V cut and face— The coach passes to players breaking out from baseline.

1 on 1 moves—(Jab step series) jab and go, jab and crossover, jab and shoot.

Group defensive slides.

Keep away—Two players 12 feet apart, defensive man in the middle, pass the ball, man in the middle puts defensive pressure on the ball, pass around him.

Two ball dribbling.

"The structure of your practice is the most determining reason for your success or lack of success as a coach." —Bob Knight

Hubie Brown offers the following practice plan template, which I added to:

*Practice Plan*

10 Min. Exercise block

10 Min. Shooting block

Big man shooting

Rapid fire shooting

Spot shooting—(off cuts and shots in offense)

| | |
|---|---|
| 10 Min. | Defensive block (2 minutes each) |
| | Build up drills—1 on 1, 2 on 2, 3 on 3, 4 on 4 |
| | Blocking out |
| | Footwork |
| | Any 5 drills you determine to use |
| 10 Min. | Offensive block |
| | Post breakdown drills |
| | 5 on 0 dummy offense |
| | Run plays |
| | Zone work |
| 15 Min. | Fast break block |
| | 2 on 1 |
| | 3 on 2 |
| | 4 on 0 |
| | 5 on 0 and 5 on 5 |
| 15 Min. | Pressure drills block (work against pressing defenses) |
| | Full court |
| | ¾ court |
| | ½ court |
| | Against traps |
| 5 Min. | Specialties |
| | Out of bounds plays |
| | Special plays |
| | Go to plays |

75 Min. total—if you have more time, then you can expand the practice.

It is important to have some practice rules because disaster will take place if you don't. My practice rules are as follows:

*Practice Rules*

1. Be early.

2. No sitting or leaning during practice.

3. Make eye contact with coach when he speaks to you.

4. Listen to all instructions.

5. Jerseys must be tucked in at all times. Every player must be in a dark color to start practice.

6. Players should not offer explanations when given direction from a coach.

7. When the whistle blows, everyone stops immediately. The balls go into the racks. No long shots.

8. No spitting on the floor.

9. Be enthusiastic. Be positive and encouraging to your fellow teammates.

10. No excuses. Keep playing.

11. No profanity.

12. Do not leave the practice floor unless you have permission from a coach.

13. Discuss any concerns you have after practice or the next day.

14. Understand that you will be expected to practice hard.

15. Practice is considered a privilege and can be taken away.

16. The only reason to miss practice would be due to an injury, a home emergency, or study purposes.

17. Have fun!

# Miscellaneous Ideas on Practice

1. Put a book of drills together that you can use for practice.

2. Move quickly from one drill to another.

3. Break down post and perimeter players for teaching specific skills and fundamentals.

4. Only go 5–7 minutes for each drill. Some drills may only take 2 minutes.

5. Plan for the most efficient use of limited time and facilities.

6. Run suicides that are timed for 30 seconds in practice.

7. The coach needs to be intense in practice.

8. Understand that teams take on the personality of their coach.

9. Make practice fun and productive.

10. Championships are won in practice.

11. Teach basketball by progression.

12. Make drills competitive.

13. Coaching is preparation.

14. Be a master teacher of the game.

15. The coach should be on the floor early for practice.

16. Have a season plan, a weekly plan, and a daily plan.

17. Understand that repetition is the key to player improvement.

18. Limit scrimmaging. It's needed but don't overdo it.

19. The coach should make an analysis of each day's practice.

20. Have a written practice plan and follow.

21. When players are in a line to run a drill, offense goes to the defense and defense goes to the end of the line.

22. Teach the whole first and then break it down.

I mention several times in this book about the importance of getting an edge. If you work hard developing an outstanding practice plan and implement that plan with creativity and enthusiasm you will attain that edge and will be using the Off-Broadway style of coaching basketball.

"Prepare practice as if Coach Calapari were coming to watch you." —Fran Franschilla

# 8 Communication

As a coach, I was always looking for new ideas and concepts that could help me improve the ways I communicated with my players. I believed that if I could do a better job communicating with my players, that I would have that edge that I was looking for.

It is my belief that the success of any coach at any level is tied to how well they communicate with their players. I don't know where the following phrase came from, but I have heard it thousands of times. "It's not what you know that counts, it's what your players know."

I was always concerned that my players understood and accepted what I was telling them. If they understood it was very obvious. But other times it was not.

I found some helpful tips online in an article by Crookes (1991) Complan Column, "Athletics Coach." He stated that coaches need to ask the following questions:

"Do I have the athlete's attention?

Am I explaining myself in an easily understood manner?

Has the athlete understood?

Does the athlete believe what I am telling him/her?

Does the athlete accept what I am saying?"

But how do you know the answers to these questions? There may be some clues that will make the coach more confident that the players are understanding and buying into what is being communicated. According to Crookes, the following actions might tip the coach off as to the player's level of understanding:

"A player's eye contact, head-nod, or facial expressions.

Body language or non-verbal signals.

Many times their faces will tell you all you need to know."

Crookes believes that difficulties in communicating with an athlete may be due to a number of issues including the following:

"1. The athlete's perception of something is different than yours.

2. The athlete may jump to a conclusion instead of working through the process of hearing, understanding, and accepting.

3. The athlete may lack the knowledge needed to understand what you are trying to communicate.

4. The athlete may lack the motivation to listen to you. The coach may have difficulty in expressing what she/he wishes to say to the athlete.

5. Emotions may interfere in the communication process. There may be a clash of personalities between you and the athlete."

Communication is the imparting or interchange of thoughts, opinions, or information by speech, writing, or signs. In my estimation, communication is the lone bastion in a basketball coach's arsenal. We study offenses and defenses and draw Xs and Os. We all line up to hear Coach Calapari talk about his Dribble Drive offense. But how to communicate with players is somewhat an untouched area, and it is my belief it is just as important or more so than learning the Xs and Os. The only basketball coach who I have heard speak on this subject is Mike Krzyzewski.

According to Coach Krzyzewski, "Effective teamwork begins and ends with communication. Communication does not always occur naturally, and must be taught and practiced in order to bring everyone together as one. The most crucial element of communicating is telling the truth."

Coach Krzyzewski lists his three best practices in communication:

1. Prioritize Listening.
2. Focus on Honesty, not Emotion.
3. Be Direct.

Coach Krzyzewski goes on to explain, "that you might think basketball programs are only concerned with two systems, offensive and defensive, dealing with the basketball "Xs and Os." However, there is a third system that our staff instills in our program—a communication system. Communication is an undercurrent that runs throughout all aspects of the program, from off-the-court meetings, conversations and film sessions to the offensive and defensive systems being run on the court during practices and games. One can see that putting a focus on having an effective communication system improves all other aspects of an organization."

As I mentioned at the beginning of this chapter, improving communication between coaches and players has always interested me. I am going to continue to study this question and maybe it might call for me to write another book.

"You hear, but do you listen!" —Unknown

# 9 Offensive Concepts

There are basically two types of coaching philosophies used when it comes to deciding what type of offense you are going to use as a coach. Are you the system type of coach or are you the flexible type of coach I mentioned in a previous chapter? Of course, much goes into developing any philosophy. Certainly the type of talent you have on your team is a factor. Another factor could be your experience as a player or coach, that determines the type of offense you are comfortable using.

The Broadway coaches are mostly teaching the same things on offense. It's all about ball screens, spacing, penetrating, kicking out, and shooting threes.

In this chapter we are *not* going to explore the different types of offenses you could use. We are going to explore the different offensive concepts you should be teaching your players.

Some coaches like Coach K. actually use a variety of offensive concepts as his basic offense. Coach K. calls concepts such as these, *actions*.

Staying with our idea of keeping things simple and not trying to digest too much, you must determine what offensive concepts are important to you and your offensive philosophy.

I will list several offensive concepts and you can pick and choose what seems to work for you and your team.

## Offensive Concepts

1. *Spacing*—Players should be 15 to 18 feet apart.

2. *Shot Selection*—This was explained in Chapter 3.

3. *Dribble with Purpose*—Dribble only to drive to the basket, advance the basketball, improve passing angle.

4. *Patience*—Some coaches believe in a four-pass mentality before you shoot. Always have patience. Defense will eventually break down.

5. *Help Someone Get Open*—screening techniques and angles.

6. *Offensive Role Definition*—Players must understand their role and how they fit into the offense.

7. *Ball Reversal*—The ball should be passed from side - top - side or reversed often.

8. *Pass Away From The Defense*—This is extremely important when passing into the post and against pressure defense.

9. *Timing*—All offenses have timing or flow to them.

10. *Inside/Out Mentality*—The best time to shoot a 3 is from the pass out of the post.

11. *Foul Shot Mentality*—Get to the foul line often through your offense.

12. *Create Offense with Defense*—This may be a reason to press, trap and cause turnovers.

13. *Involve Pick and Roll in Your Offense*—This is a difficult play to defend with man defense.

14. *Tempo*—How fast or how slow are you going to play?

15. *Offensive Repetition*—Whatever concepts must be practiced over and over.

16. *Don't Play Point Guard from The Middle of the Floor*—Point guard must dribble toward the wing to start offense.

17. *Slipping Screens*—Teach slipping screens, on or off the ball.

18. *Anti-Switching Concept*—Teach your players what to do if the defense switches screens. The best way is to slip screens, set consecutive screens, and use a third player in pick and roll.

19. *Zone Offense Concepts*—Penetrate, skip pass, screen, post stay behind defense, shot fake and pass fake. Emphasize: Fake Pass/ Make Pass!

20. *Floor Balance*—Determine how many players you want back on defense. Usually one or two players. Point guard should always be back.

21. *Offensive Rebound*—This should be considered part of your offense. Get second and third shots. Rebound opposite the shot. 69% of shots rebound opposite.

22. *Moving Without the Ball*—Players must read the defense and learn how to get open.

23. *Passing*—Teach different kinds of passes, especially against defensive pressure. Eliminate passing turnovers: Make the safe pass!

24. *Executing the "V" Cut*—The offensive player should take his defender in one direction and then move quickly in another direction as the screener is moving into position.

25. *Step And Go*—Step the defender out, plant your outside foot and cut to the basket. (Backdoor move.)

26. *Square Up To the Basket*—The player receiving the pass should always square to the basket and get into a triple threat position so that the player can shoot/pass/dribble.

27. *Alignment*—This is how you set up your players to start the offense. For example: 4 perimeter players and one post man. (4 @ 1)

28. *Entry*—This is how you enter the ball to start your offense.

29. *Post Feeds*—In my estimation it is very important in any offense to get the ball inside, even if you want to kick it back out to shoot a three.

It has always been my belief that it really doesn't matter what offense you use if it is based on solid offensive principles and concepts. You will be able to research what offense you would like to use by using the internet or by looking at the many DVDs that are out there on offensive schemes. Some of the offenses that you might consider are as follows:

1. Motion
2. Flex
3. Triangle
4. Princeton
5. Ball Screen (High or side)
6. Dribble Drive
7. Open Post

Some offenses are based on continuity and others are based on different screening sets or cutting actions. Some coaches just like to run set plays or quick hitters. You will need to develop your zone offense to fit your system as well. Also, there are fast break schemes and secondary or early offense ideas to choose from if you want to include them in your offense.

No matter what offense you choose to use with your team, teaching the offensive concepts is a must.

"Create unselfishness as the most important team attribute." —Bill Russell

# 10 Defensive Concepts

I received my man-to-man defensive education while I was a graduate assistant at Ohio University. One of the assistant coaches and my mentor, Mike Schuler, had been an assistant under Coach Bob Knight when he was coaching at Army.

I have used Bob Knight's defensive concepts throughout my coaching career and I believe that it is the single most reason for my coaching success. When Coach Knight began using his pressure man-to-man defense it was a revolution. And of course, his defensive concepts spread like wildfire throughout the basketball coaching world and they are still used to this day.

I believe that choosing your defensive concepts is quite different than choosing your offensive concepts. There is a large array of offensive concepts that are not necessarily connected to one another. That is not true with the defensive concepts. There is somewhat of a connection between all the defensive concepts. The reason for that is most of the concepts must work together before a defensive stop can occur. It's very similar to the domino effect. Tip the first domino and they all fall in order.

As I have mentioned several times in this book, I am a proponent of using man-to-man defense in youth basketball. My philosophy is that man-to-man defense should be used as the primary defense from the junior varsity team and down to fourth grade, community, CYO, and AAU basketball.

What some coaches don't understand is that even though your team is playing man-to-man defense, there are many zone principles that are used. Man-to-man defense is actually a combination of zone and man-to-man principles. But even if you decide to use a zone defense with your team, the man-to-man defensive concepts need to be taught. If not, your zone defense will not be as effective.

What I found out coaching Off-Broadway basketball was that I needed to adjust my man-to-man defense almost every year depending on the talent and defensive intelligence of my players. Some years I could put a lot of pressure on the ball, or play a pressure defense, while other years I had to play a sagging or pack-line defense. Some years I could switch and other years I couldn't. As I mentioned before, one of the traits of Off-Broadway basketball is that things are always changing. In order to be successful I had to be willing to change my defense from year to year.

## Defensive Concepts

1. *Ball Side*—this is the side of the court that the ball is on. (Pressure side)

2. *Help Side*—this is the side of the court away from the ball. (Help stop the ball)

3. *Ball Pressure*—The cornerstone of all man-to-man defense. The defensive player should be positioned on the basketball so he or she is close enough to touch his or her shirt. (If a player picks up his dribble, the defensive player should move in tight with both hands up.)

4. *Ball You Man*—The defensive player is positioned between man and ball. The defensive player should maintain this position at all times when you are not guarding the ball.

5. *On The Line/Up The Line*—The position of the players who are not guarding the person with the ball.

6. *Jump To The Ball*—When the ball is passed, all defensive players should move in the direction of the pass.

7. *Vision*—See the ball and the person you are guarding. Vision of the ball is of the utmost importance. Point to the player you are guarding and the ball (Pistols).

8. *Communication*—Talking on defense is a must. Must be practiced and different terms developed to have a consistent communication system.

9. *50/50 Balls*—These are loose balls from fumbles, deflections, rebounds, or any other situation where there is no possession of the ball by either team in live action. The team should strive to get at least 70% of these loose balls.

10. *Defensive Help*—All players not guarding the ball must be alert to stop the penetration of the basketball either by the dribble or the pass.

11. *Help The Helper*—Helping on defense results in a defensive rotation whereas defensive players cover the player or players that the helper left.

12. *Help And Recover*—Stopping the penetration of the basketball by leaving your assigned player and then recovering back to that player.

13. *Transition Defense*—After a change in the possession of the basketball players must convert from offense to defense and get back. Must be practiced. I consider this to be the most important defensive concept.

14. *Practice Preparation*—Practice how to defend every offensive situation including cuts, screens, ball screens, actions, and common offenses.

15. *Deflections*—Keep stats on how many deflections your team makes on defense. A deflection is whatever the coach wants it to be, but usually tipping the ball or just getting a finger tip on the ball counts. You could include blocked shots, charges, caused loose balls, and steals as a deflection as other examples. College teams want to get 30–35 deflections per game.

16. *Defend Ball Screens*—This must be practiced daily. There are several ways to defend the ball screen such as: (1) switching, (2) hedging (person guarding screener jumps out and tries to stop ball, as the ball defender gets over the screen, then switches back), (3) going under the screen.

17. *Post Defense*—Never allow a post player to beat you. Double team the post if the opponent has an outstanding offensive post player or choke the post by having perimeter defensive players collapse on the post.

# Blocking Shots

Something that I learned later on in my coaching career was the tremendous value of blocking shots to your defense. I always talked about how important taking charges was, but as the rules have changed on the block/charge, officials don't call many charges anymore. In fact about 80% of charge attempts are called against you, as a block. Plus there was always the risk of getting players injured taking charges. So I began to emphasize blocking shots. It is great if you have a big athletic leaper who can block shots, but what I learned was that even guards could be taught to block shots if you practiced it.

Even if your team does not have the traditional shot blocker, it is possible to still get those blocked shots and they make a big difference in your defense. It's like anything else. If you work on it in practice you can have success blocking shots. The most important factor is that you make your team believe that they can block shots. Two or three blocked shots in a game can make a tremendous difference in your opponents shooting percentage.

For example: Using 60 possessions per game, here is an idea on how many blocked shots per game would really affect the game. (Of course if you had fewer possessions, it would take less blocks to affect the game.)

## Blocked Shots

| *Average* | *Good* | *Excellent* |
|---|---|---|
| 6% or 3.6 blocks per game = 3.6 fewer shots | 8% or 4.8 blocks per game = 4.8 fewer shots | 10% or 6 blocks per game = 6.0 fewer shots |

If a team shot 45% for the game and you blocked 4 shots, the blocked shots would reduce that shooting percentage down to 43.2. If a team shot 45% for the game and you blocked 5 shots, the blocked shots would reduce that shooting percentage down to 42.7%. And if a team shot 45% for the game and you blocked 6 shots, the blocked shots would reduce that shooting percentage down to 42.3%.

## Teaching Points

1. Go across the arm—outside hand and arm used to block shot.

2. Keep your body balanced and on the balls of your feet ready to react and move in any direction at any moment in time.

3. Keep your hands up about eye level or higher but not fully extended until the ball is actually released by the shooter.

4. Keep your body parallel to the attacking player and giving them space which also lets you react with less chance of having a foul called.

5. Accept that altering a shot for a miss is just as beneficial as physically blocking the shot.

6. If you must block a ball where you cannot get your body between your player and the penetrating player, chase the player and attempt to block the ball from behind by reaching with your inside arm over the outside shoulder of the offensive player. This lets them release the ball and allows you to block the shot on the upward flight, avoiding body contact.

"The difference between a good defensive team and a bad defensive team is as little as three possessions." —Brad Stevens

## Individual Defensive Concepts

1. Watch the belly button.

2. On the ball—use reach step.

3. Stance—sit down, head in center of body.

4. Close out—hard on your man, hands up, chop feet.

5. Don't reach in.

6. Don't foul.

7. Denial—deny him or her the basketball, one pass away from ball.

8. Defend the post—(1) play behind, (2) total front, (3) three quarters high side.

9. First priority on defense is the ball.

10. Eliminate all easy baskets and force your opponent to shoot contested shots.

11. Hands up on all shots.

12. Intelligent ball pressure—give a cushion if needed.

13. Help early.

14. Balance is important on defense—head in center of body.

15. Use peripheral vision.

16. Gang rebound.

17. Every defensive player must work together.

18. Keep your body between your man and the basket.

19. Cover down—get to the level of the ball on dribble or pass penetration.

20. Always be ready to help your teammate.

21. Be aware.

22. Think blocked shot.

23. Those players who can guard multiple positions are very valuable to your defense.

# 11 Motivational Techniques for Teaching Defense

The Broadway programs are going to have quicker players, bigger players, smarter players, more athletic players, more agile players, and players that are motivated by big crowds, to play defense. But in no way does this mean that you can't have your team be a good defensive team. You can motivate your team to play defense just as well or better than Coach K. or Coach Cal.

One of the things I have learned over the years about coaching defense is that it is not enough for your players to know the individual and team defensive concepts, but that you must motivate your players to play the type of defense that wins games. If you can motivate and convince your team to play aggressive defense, your chances of winning increase immensely.

As has been noted several times in other chapters, it is my belief that man-to-man defense should be used when coaching youth teams. The fundamentals of man-to-man or person-to-person defense should be learned when your players are young.

There are two parts to having an outstanding defensive team. One is to make sure that your team understands the defensive principles of the defense that you are teaching, whether it be man-to-man or zone. Second is to *motivate* players to play great defense on a consistent basis. Without a doubt *motivation* is the key. There are five principles I have learned about motivation and defense:

1. A coach must get players out of their comfort zone to play great defense.
2. There is a certain defensive mindset that must be developed.
3. Defense must be sold to the players constantly.
4. Coaches must arouse players' competitive desires to be successful defensively.
5. Defense requires constant motivation.

There are two types of motivation that are important for teaching defense. They are:

*Intrinsic motivation*—Which is motivation from within. Meeting goals and developing pride are important to this type of motivation.

*Extrinsic motivation*—Which is motivation coming from a source outside. Tangible rewards such as trophies, medals, etc. and praise and recognition are important to this type of motivation.

"Coaches who can outline plays on a blackboard are a dime a dozen. The ones who win, get inside their players and motivate."
—Vince Lombardi

## Motivational Philosophy of Defense

In order to be successful in motivating players to play defense, coaches must have a philosophy of approach. My philosophy of motivating defensive play is as follows:

1. Develop a full-time organized campaign to sell defense to players, fans, and media.

2. Develop a defensive attitude within each player.

3. Build a defensive tradition. Make it something players can pass on.

4. Create a tone for your defense by using aggressive defensive drills.

5. Develop a name for your defense. (Examples: No Name Defense, Orange Crush, SWAT Team, Mosquito Defense, Belly Button Defense.)

6. Award and reward defensive effort. (Examples: game balls, trophies, pats on the back, single out a player to the media.)

## Knight/Krzyzewski Teaching Methods

Professor Scott Snook of the Harvard Business School teaches a class in leadership in which he compares the leadership and teaching methods of Bobby Knight and Mike Krzyzewski. Professor Snook starts out the class with a question: "Is it better to be loved or feared?"

Of course Bobby Knight used discipline and intimidation in his teaching methods. It was a tough-love approach.

On the opposite end, Mike Krzyzewski used positive reinforcement and open and warm communication.

*So which of the two teaching methods would be best for motivating players to play defense?*

The results are similar. Both coaches have always had outstanding defensive teams. There is no doubt that Knight's approach is out of favor in this day and age. However, Coach Knight's approach can still be effective. And if you talk to players who have played for Knight, most say they love the man.

Professor Snook believes your feelings about people have a lot to do with what type of coach you will be. He believes if you think people are fundamentally bad and normally try to get over and get by, you will probably use the Knight approach. However, if you believe people are fundamentally good and are self-motivated and always try to do their best, then you are going to use the Coach K. approach.

Professor Snook does make a very important point and that is the "situation" at the time may determine what type of teaching method you may use. So there may be times when the two methods are mixed.

"Our chief in life is someone who shall make us do what we can." —Ralph Waldo Emerson

## Evaluation of Defensive Play

You can't always determine how well your team is playing defense by the number of points that your opponent scores. Other factors sometimes such as pace of play can be the determining factor. In Chapter 1 on "Statistical Edge," I explained the method of using the Defensive Efficiency Rating system. If you remember our defensive goal of .75 DER gives us the best evaluation of how well we played defense. However I believe that there are some other ways of evaluating your defense, such as:

1. By developing a defensive grade sheet. You can evaluate transition defense, positioning, effort, block outs, on ball defense, off ball defense, ball pressure, help side, and stopping penetration.

2. By adding extra columns to your stat sheet. I have added three columns to my individual player stat sheet: (1) points you allowed, (2) give-up penetration, (3) shots allowed.

3. By developing an efficiency chart like the one I described in Chapter 1: Statistical Edge, in which there are pluses and minuses for defensive play.

4. By using the Defensive Efficiency Ratings System (DER) which is simply possessions divided into points scored.

"The most important defensive statistic to me is field goal percentage." —Roy Williams

## Setting Defensive Goals

I've always felt that goal setting is important in the game of basketball, both individual and team. Defensive goals (individual and team) are a must if your defense is going to be successful. The following are the defensive goals I used when I coached at the college level. You may need to adjust them to your level of play. For example, for my junior high eighth grade team, I used 30 points given up per game.

*A. College Team Goals*

1. Limit opponents to 65 points per game.
2. Limit opponents to 42% on two point shots.
3. Limit opponents to 25% from the three-points line.
4. Force opponents into 24 turnovers.
5. Limit opponents free throws to 15.
6. Have at least 30+ deflections.
7. Don't permit an individual player to score 20 points in a game.

*B. Individual Goals*

1. Individual defensive goals need to be broken down by position—post players, guards, and wings. For example: post players limit a certain number of touches in the post, or guards/wings limit a certain number of penetrations. This is something you can be creative with and you can highlight the important things in your defensive philosophy.

## Defensive Leadership Plan

I heard a coach by the name of Maury John from Drake University speak at a clinic many years ago and I took some of his points with some of mine and developed a "Defensive Leadership Plan." It has been the basis for building the tough defense that I like to play.

1. Determine a defensive leader. This player can have all the great defensive traits such as quickness and speed, or he may be a player with tremendous desire.

2. Hold private meetings with the defensive leader. Talk philosophy, team defense, individual defense, etc., make the leader feel important and needed.

3. Make leader "Chairman of Defense Department." (Defense motivation emphasis must come from a player as well as a coach.)

4. Give chairman a defensive notebook (the only player to have one).

5. Allow chairman to demonstrate and teach defensive principles. He will act as an assistant coach on defense.

6. The chairman wears a "Chairman of Defense Department" tee shirt before practice and during warm-ups (only player to have one).

## Miscellaneous Ideas For Teaching Defense

Here are some other ideas to motivate team members to play defense:

Bring outside sources in to present to players the importance of defense. We have used college coaches, films, and former players.

Teach whole method in practice, then break it down. It is easier for players to relate to what a coach wants them to do.

Use gimmicks to help motivate players. I have used slogans such as, "If you don't play 'D' you'll be on the 'B'" and if a player is exceptional at help side defense I call him "Mr. Clean" and give him a bottle of Mr. Clean Detergent. I have stamped the back of all players hands with the defensive goal for a particular game. I have also selected a "Defensive Player of the Week" and put their picture in the cafeteria for the week.

Allow players in defensive drills to defend only 15 or 20 seconds. In a game situation this is the most time they will be playing defense at any one time. It builds confidence.

Explain the reason why we do certain things on defense.

Basketball is a game of courage, especially on defense.

On the first day of practice, throw all of the balls out of the gym and lock the doors. Do nothing but defensive positioning drills.

It is very important to use teachable moments when practicing defense.

Try to create an atmosphere where the team has such a tight bond with each other and play for each other, they don't need you.

Video data is a good way for players to see themselves and correct flaws on defense.

Players must get out of their comfort zone. You must get them to be comfortable with being uncomfortable.

Newton's Second Law states that an object will accelerate in the direction you push it. You must push them on defense.

I have used the term Lockdown Defender in describing just how we want to play individual defense.

Implement your defensive goals in practice, constantly call attention to them.

Make sure your players understand that gambling on defense is a risk.

"The best way to be a great motivator is to get rid of those who don't want to be motivated." —Lou Holtz

# 33.9 Defense

During 1968–69, Ashland University set a NCAA single season record of only allowing 33.9 points per game. The coach of that team was a highly intense gentlemen by the name of Bill Musselman. He wrote a book entitled *33.9 Defense*. At Ashland University, his pre-game warm up was like a circus. He had a Harlem Globetrotter type of warm up, with juggling basketballs, players riding unicycles, and many other bizarre basketball activities. Coach Musselman later became the head basketball coach at the University of Minnesota, and head coach of several NBA teams, including the Cleveland Cavaliers.

Bill Musselman was probably one of the best motivators of playing defense than any coach I had ever seen, including Bob Knight. In his book *33.9 Defense*, he stated that his goal was to one day coach a game where he shut out the other team on defense. He wanted to have the opponent score ZERO points. As a way of motivation he told his team that on an almost daily basis. He believed that each defensive possession was like a war and had to be won. Musselman got into quite a bit of trouble while he was coaching at the University of Minnesota when he was quoted as saying, "Defeat is worse than death, because you have to live with defeat." That quote was given credit for establishing the foundation of attitude of his University of Minnesota team, the team that was involved in a fierce fight during a game with Ohio State.

Regardless of that terrible fight with Ohio State in 1971–72, I always believed that Bill Musselman was one of the best motivational teachers of defense that we have ever seen.

It is important to remember that we must motivate daily, and teaching and motivating defensive play is a selling effort. I think we all realize that games are won on the practice floor, and you must give yourself every opportunity to be the best defensive team that you can be, providing that your philosophy is to be a great defensive team.

# 12 Understanding Offensive Strategic Coaching

I began to really understand the concept of "Offensive Strategic Coaching" my last couple of years of coaching. It's a simple concept, but I had trouble recognizing it because I was busy worrying about my half court offense. I learned it's very important for a coach to know where and how the points are being scored for his/her team.

I never thought to actually analyze where the points were coming from or how we were scoring our points. I was aware if we got a basket on a play, or if we scored on a fast break, or if we scored on transition. But I really wasn't looking at it in an analytical way.

I started studying this whole idea of how we were scoring our points. The first thing that I had to develop was a recognition of how we were actually scoring our points. For example:

1. Did we score off a set play?
2. Did we score off a broken play?
3. Did we score on a fast break?
4. Did we score on an unstructured play?
5. Did we score on transition?

Consequently, I had to be proficient in knowing what was a structured play and what was an unstructured play. Of course, I had to look at our "game video" and break it down and be able to "label" each scoring possession. Depending on what level you are coaching, you may not have the luxury of even having your games recorded. So it might be that just understanding this concept will give you insight into what is possibly happening offensively with your team. If you had the manpower you could have someone keep stats on how your team scores.

What I found out with my research changed my preparation, practice time, and emphasis on offensive basketball.

After I accumulated my information, I went on the internet to see if I could find any other research. The only information I could find was from Ron Ekker who did a program through "Basketball Talk Pro" called "The Third Element—Silver Bullet."

One of Coach Ekker's concepts on this subject was to use the 80/20 rule to explain where he thought the points were coming from. But instead of 80/20 he estimated it should be 70/30. Coach Ekker broke it down in the following manner:

"1. 30% of the points will be scored in structured play.

2. 70% of the points will be scored in unstructured play."

Coach Ekker defined structured play and unstructured play in the following manner:

"*Structured Play*

1. Plays

2. Out-of-bounds Plays

3. Secondary Fast Break Plays

*Unstructured Play*

1. Fast Break

2. Transition—Improvised play
3. Play Breakdown
4. No Play—Pick-up Play"

If a team scored 100 points in a game as an example:
70 points would be scored in unstructured play.
30 points would be scored in structured play.

Coach Ekker also highlighted some other terminology in explaining his concept of the "Third Element—Silver Bullet" theory:

"1. Fast Break—Any basket scored in four to six seconds
2. Random Plays—Run without coach's direction
    A. Pick & Roll
    B. Give & Go
3. Recognizing a miss-match—Unstructured play
4. Offensive rebound
5. Pass out to perimeter from post
6. Improvising is always unstructured play"

I was always very meticulous in preparing practice plans for offensive play. I believed in drills, offensive breakdown drills, and even going 5 on 0 running offensive plays, as well as 5 on 5. But what about the unstructured play? What was I doing to work on that 70% of my scoring offense?

# Coaching Ugly

I coined a phrase that I never believed I would ever think about doing: *Coaching Ugly.* I was always so proud of my practice plans and from time to time I would get compliments on what great practices we ran; how organized, how detailed they were. Now was I just going to "roll-the-ball-out" and *Coach Ugly*? I was conflicted knowing that 70% of my offense was coming from "unstructured play," and spending most of my offensive practice time on structured play. I decided to spend at least some of my practice time on unstructured play, *Coaching Ugly!*

I had to make some adjustments to my practices if I was going to *Coach Ugly.* As a result, I developed the following ideas:

1. I had to let go and not be afraid to *Coach Ugly.*
2. Believe that players learn better by actually playing the game.
3. I thought that short bursts (2–5 minutes) of unstructured play was better because that is usually how it occurred in games.
4. A greater emphasis on "carry over" from practice to games.
5. Include more competition in drills.
6. Creating more game-like environments in practice.
7. Do everything full-court (94 feet).
8. Use practice time daily on 1-on-1 drills and "Jab Step Series."
9. Spend practice time each day on 2-on-2 and 3-on-3 unstructured play.

According to Coach John Carrier on his Coaching Basketball Blog, "The hardest part for you as the coach is going to be giving up control and letting guys just learn from playing. It's not going to be pretty, but boy it is effective."

Also, according to Brian McCormick in his book *The 21st Century Basketball Practice*, "The game of basketball has evolved over the last generation, but basketball practices have changed very little during my 30 years in the game as a player, coach, clinician, and consultant. Today's game more closely resembles the game that we played on the playground than the one we're taught in practice."

What a profound statement by Coach McCormick. I am 100% in agreement with him. Of course there are some reasons for this. The shot clock and 3 point shot has brought a lot of it on, but I basically think it is the way players are brought up playing the game today.

Coach McCormick goes on to explain in his book, "that tremendous amounts of learning occurred on the playgrounds and during pick-up games for people of a certain generation, and players today often miss the learning to attend organized practices or sessions with a skill trainer."

It was very difficult for me to "let loose," but I believe that this whole concept of "Offensive Strategic Coaching," and *Coaching Ugly*, made our teams better and I believe our players enjoyed playing more with this system. However, using this system was just a small part of my practice plan, I still believed in a structured practice with break-down drills, running set plays, and doing things in a controlled manner. But the *Coaching Ugly* phase of practice was considered to be a very important part of the practice plan.

# 13 Social Media and The Internet

This is an area where I think the Off-Broadway coach may have a better situation than the Broadway coach, and that is dealing with social media. Can you imagine what that is like for a program like Kentucky, dealing with all the social media? It has to be a nightmare for the coaches. However, no matter what level you are coaching social media is a factor and coaches need to take advantage of it.

It is my belief that the basketball coach who does not use responsible social media as part of his coaching responsibilities is making a huge mistake. Long gone are the days when coaching was just communicating eyeball to eyeball with your players. Your players live in a different world of communication than most of us did. With all the options of social media, no matter what level you coach, there is no excuse not to take advantage of this fantastic medium. The eighth grade junior high players I coached were definitely connected to social media. Every one of them owned a cell phone and many carried laptop computers.

Most schools have policies concerning the use of social media, and you as the coach should also have your rules and regulations in how social media is used. Monitoring by the school and the coach is also important. But, if used responsibly, social media can be a very valuable tool in communicating with players and parents, as well as another tool to help your players learn the game of basketball.

Childress Sports recommends that you develop social media training for your athletes that go beyond the normal Dos and Don'ts. Childress Sports believes that, "student-athletes can 'win' with social media—if given the right tools, through a 'Social Media Workshop.'" This workshop can help the student-athlete by:

1. Building strategies for use.
2. Developing a personal brand.
3. Learning how to avoid communication blunders.
4. Recognizing social media opportunities.
5. Discovering how to use social media to enhance the brands of school, athletic department, and team.

My recommendation would be to make sure that you outline how you are going to use social media with your athletic director or person in charge of the program. I believe it is important to make sure they sign off on your use of this technology with the team and parents.

There are so many examples of how powerful social media has become in this day and age. For example: Pete Carroll of the Seattle Seahawks uses social media to build fan loyalty, and John Calipari of the University of Kentucky has over a million Twitter fans with whom he communicates. When LeBron James played for the Miami Heat, they had more fans on their Facebook page than any other NBA team. Also, the Heat used social media to promote their "Heat Youth Basketball Clinic." The Heat also uses Facebook to build enthusiasm for the team by posting weekly highlights of the past few games.

## Social Media Options

*Facebook*

Facebook has a wide range of pages concerning coaching basketball. You can obtain regular updates whenever a new post or comment is made.

*Twitter*

Twitter is a type of social media that allows coaches to follow other people of interest. Twitter has a limitation where the posts have to be in 140 characters or less.

*LinkedIn*

LinkedIn has over 41 million users worldwide. It is a useful tool for business professionals. It is a great networking opportunity for coaches. Important for contacting other coaches.

*Instagram*

Capture and share the world's moments with Instagram. It is a fast way to share your life and easy way to use pictures.

*YouTube*

You can share videos with friends, family, and the world. It is a great source for finding multi-media presentations on all things related to basketball.

There are some other social media tools, but I think the ones mentioned above work best for the basketball coach. Social media is a very useful tool, but remember it must be used properly. You don't have to use all of the social media tools, but explore them and see which ones meet your needs.

## The Internet

If I had had the internet when I started coaching I would not have been limited to using the book *Power Basketball* by Ed Jucker as my bible and guide. It was the only thing that I could turn to at that time. Books were about the only way I could learn about offenses and defenses. At that time, there were not many basketball clinics, if any, and there were no videos to purchase. But today you can research just about any phase of the game of basketball through the internet.

All you need to do now is Google whatever you are interested in learning. How to attack a 1-3-1 zone defense, how to break a 1-2-1-1 full court press, or how to teach the fundamentals of man-to-man defense are on the internet and much, much more. I can't even imagine how much better a coach I would have been then if the internet had been around. It should be your most valuable tool in coaching the game of basketball.

Also, the social media that was talked about earlier has many avenues of finding and showing you with video a certain phase of the game. For instance, YouTube is very valuable in seeing the offense or defense right on video. I like the following websites, but there are many:

www.coachesclipboard.net (Drills, offenses, defenses, etc.)
www.basketballcoach.com (Drills, tips for coaching)
www.coachingtoolbox.net (Drills, offenses, defenses, etc.)
www.breakthroughbasketball.com (Coaching philosophy & drills)
www.basketballhq.com (Learning about all aspects of basketball)
www.hooptactics.com (Emphasis on offenses & defenses)
www.functionalbasketballcoaching.com (Learning opportunities)
www.mrbasketball.net ("Nitty-Gritty Basketball," basketball tips and help)
www.goxavier.com/newsletter

## Basketball Coaching Apps

If you go to the Play Store on your smart phone and type in Basketball Coaching you will get many free basketball coaching apps. Here are a few of my favorites:

1. *Assistant Basketball Coach*—The drill section is an in-depth catalog of drills for individuals and/or teams to improve the skill set of the user.

2. *Youth Basketball Drills*—Has a lot of free videos that will help you to perform good basketball drills.

3. *Basketball Shooting*—This app teaches you correct form and then gives you drills that simulate game like situations to practice.

4. *Basketball Stats Keeper*—Stats tracker program enables scorekeepers and parents to record player stats and view or share them online at Scoutlit.com.

5. *Hudl Technique*—Improve your skills through slow motion video analysis.

There are a plethora of free apps to choose from and many of them can help you with planning practices, choosing drills, drawing plays, keeping statistics, individual improvement, etc. I believe it is a very valuable tool for any basketball coach at any level.

Using the internet is a lot of common sense. I am not a skilled computer person, but I have been able to use the internet to my advantage for coaching the game of basketball. So I know you will be able to use it, I am sure, to a much greater advantage than I have.

According to the "Functional Basketball Coaching" web site, "To get the most out of your basketball coaching, one very important activity will be your ability to find 'Learning Opportunities.' Focusing on the craft or art of basketball coaching helps you push your knowledge and skill boundaries. This type of activity increases your understanding on how to do things and become a more knowledgeable coach in general."

## Social Networking Policy Used in College

Men's basketball players should always be concerned with any behavior that might embarrass themselves, their families, their team, and/or school. This includes any activities that the players conduct online.

As a men's basketball player, you are a representative of the school and are always in the public eye. Please keep the following guideline in mind as you participate on social networking web sites.

Before participating in any online community, understand that anything posted online is available to anyone in the world. Any text or photo placed online is completely out of your control the moment it is placed online—even if you limit access to your site.

You should not post information, photos, or other items online that could embarrass you, your family, your team, the athletic department or the school.

You should not post your home address, local address, phone number(s), birth date, or other personal information as well as your whereabouts or your plans. You could be opening yourself up to predators.

Men's basketball coaches and athletic department administrators can and do monitor these web sites.

Potential employers, internship supervisors, graduate programs and scholarship committees now search these sites to screen candidates and applications.

The malicious use of online social networks such as derogatory language about any member of the school community, demeaning statements about or threats to any third party, and incriminating photos or statements depicting hazing, sexual harassment, vandalism, stalking, underage drinking, illegal drug use or other inappropriate behavior will be subject disciplinary action by the Head Coach and/or Director of Athletics., if they gain knowledge of such violations. Sanctions may include written notification requiring that the unacceptable content be removed, temporary suspension from the team, dismissal from the team.

Failure to agree and adhere to this policy can result in actions ranging from reprimand or suspension to dismissal from the program. It is the Men's Basketball Program's intention to achieve a level of behavior that reflects positively on all of us.

# 14 How Do You Get Them To Play Together?

Pat Riley, in his book *The Winner Within,* published by Berkley Press (October 1, 1994), developed the terminology, "The Disease of Me," which simply means selfishness. Riley breaks "The Disease of Me" down into understandable parts, such as:

"1. Players develop an overpowering belief in their own importance.

2. Players think 'I'm the one!'

3. The greater a single teammate's success, the stronger the resentment will be.

4. 'The Disease of Me' can cause cliques, hurt feelings, and petty jealousies.

5. 'The Disease of Me' can create hidden agendas."

However, the good news is, "while it is ever present, it can be overcome," according to Riley. And I believe that is true and have experienced great success in getting rid of "The Disease of Me." But you must constantly work at it, and you have to be very careful that just because you are winning, that "The Disease of Me" is not present, because it will re-surface just when you least expect it.

It's all about getting the players to *Buy In.* You have to convince them that the success of the team is all that is important, and that their individual goals and accomplishments must come second. This is not easy to do!

Of course selfishness usually includes the following types of behavior of the player:

1. Taking a lot of shots, particular bad shots or shooting when another player has a better shot.
2. Unwilling to pass the basketball.
3. Refusing to play hard and especially on the defensive end.
4. Getting upset when taken out of the game.
5. Always checking the stat sheet to see how many points scored.

The plan that I instituted to combat selfishness is as follows:

1. First, I explain to the players that basketball is not an equal opportunity sport. Everyone doesn't have to shoot or score.
2. At a team meeting, I ask the team who the best shooter on the team is, and then the second best shooter, and then the third best, and so on.
3. I explain that when they shoot the basketball it is a team shot, not an individual shot.
4. I explain to them that they don't have to score to be a good basketball player. Defense, rebounding, making assists, doing the little things, like setting screens, etc. are as important as scoring.
5. I ask them if they would rather average 20 points per game and win 10 games, or average 10 points per game and win 20 games.

6. I explain to them that we want the best shooters shooting the ball and that I am not trying to make anyone a star, but giving us the best chance to win the game.

7. I ask them to make the extra pass to *Trust the Pass.*

8. I then explain that selfishness is human nature, but that we must overcome that human frailty and we will work all season to get rid of selfishness.

9. I explain to the players that they must sacrifice to be a member of the team. You must give up something—recognition, awards, etc., to get something even better.

10. The players must understand that our success will come through unselfishness.

## Superman Award

"*Superman who had powers and abilities far beyond those of mortal men, who could leap tall buildings in a single bound, race a speeding bullet to its target, and bend steel with his bare hands, devoted his existence on Earth to helping others.*"

I put together the Superman Award which highlighted unselfish play. This award was based on stats outside the normal stat sheet. Such as (1) diving on the floor after a loose ball, (2) defensive deflections, (3) unusual outstanding plays, (4) taking charges, (5) defensive plays of the game, and (6) outstanding effort to save a ball going out of bounds. You can make these stats anything that you would want. We announced the Superman Award at the next practice after a game, when we gathered at center court at the end of practice.

This award was part of my plan to help destroy selfishness. To focus on unselfish play and to give credit and meaning to something other than "how many points did you score tonight?"

According to Trevor McLean in his article "How to Easily Stop Selfishness in Basketball," there seems to be three major reasons why players develop a selfish attitude:

"1. Society has conditioned young people to be selfish.

2. The factor of trust—players don't trust their teammates.

3. Individual is searching for approval—consequently drawing attention to himself or herself."

Coach McLean believes that the best way to teach unselfishness is to first do the following:

"1. Try and prevent it from the start of the season.

2. Take the player out of the game and have a quick word with him/her.

3. Talk to the player privately.

4. Constantly praise players who are unselfish.

5. Last but not least, is to show the player the *bench*."

I have had to use more severe tactics from time to time with a player who simply will not conform to our ideas of unselfishness. Such as: doing sprints, being thrown out of practice, suspension from the team, or even expulsion from the team. Those things are last resort tactics but sometimes there is very little choice because, "one bad apple may spoil the barrel."

According to John Wooden in his book *Practical Modern Basketball*, teamwork means the following: "We want no 'one-man' players, no 'stars.' One player attempting to 'grandstand' can wreck the best team ever organized. The team is first, individual credit is second. There is no place for selfishness, egotism, or envy on our team."

However, in teaching unselfish basketball play to your players, they must understand that a player who shoots a lot and scores a lot of points is not necessarily a selfish player. Sometimes that player is automatically labeled a selfish player, which is not always true.

"Shine your stars, work your horses, fix your problems, get rid of deadwood." —SMU Basketball

"When a gifted team dedicates itself to unselfish trust and combines instinct with boldness and effort, it is ready to climb." —Pat Riley

# 15 How Do You Get Them to Play Hard?

My teams always played "hard." It was something that I expected out of them and I accepted no excuses for not playing hard. There is a large range of philosophies as far as getting your players to play hard. There are those coaches that scream and yell and punish the team if they don't play hard. And there are those coaches that use motivation and psychology to get their players to play hard. As a coach, I used a little bit of each of those philosophies.

I always told my players, "Don't make me coach effort!" The idea I was trying to create with that statement was that it is your responsibility as a player to play hard and I as the coach should not have to be concerned with making you play hard. However, understand that you can't make anyone do anything, they have to want to do it.

Don Kelbick, in his article, "Getting Your Basketball Team to Play Hard," listed four factors in getting your team to play hard. They are:

"1. *Connect with your players*—Show them that you care about them and that you have interest in them.

2. *Be Positive*—It is more productive to push people toward something as opposed to pulling them.

3. *Be Consistent*—The players have to know what you will accept and what you won't. If your standards and reaction change from day to day players become confused and resentful.

4. *Preach Success*—The greatest motivation is success. Players will do anything if you can convince them they will be successful."

According to Craig Moody, in his article entitled, "Learning to Play Hard: The Number One Skill in Basketball," "playing hard all the time can easily be considered the number one skill in basketball and provides the key to unlocking a player's potential." Coach Moody believes that playing hard has a tremendous amount of benefits for the player and the team. Here are some of those benefits:

"1. Playing hard is the players key to unlocking their potential.

2. Playing hard often intimidates opponents.

3. Playing hard is leading by example.

4. Playing hard by nature makes you more alert.

5. Playing hard tells your coach and your teammates you are 100% committed and they can count on you.

6. Playing hard is mentally tough and requires a high level of concentration."

One of the themes that I used to get our players to play hard was to keep telling them that we want to be the "hardest working team in the country." I told them that we wanted to outwork everyone in sight. I kept telling them to go the extra mile and leave it all on the court.

I think you get players to play hard also by building a culture. You make it part of the culture and players feel that it is just something that they must do. It is expected and they understand that we are a part of something bigger than ourselves. "When it's part of your culture, it doesn't have to be articulated," says Miles Plumlee, Duke University's team captain in 2011–12. "It's always been part of everything we do from the day we stepped in the gym."

Jay Bilas in his book *Toughness* talked about hearing that, "Coach Knight had criticized a player of his by saying, 'You just want to be comfortable out there!' Well, that was me, and when I heard that, it clicked with me. I needed to work to increase my capacity for work, not to make it easier to play. I needed to work in order to be more productive in my time on the floor. Tough players play so hard that their coaches have to take them out to get rest so they can put them back in. The toughest players don't pace themselves."

From time to time in my coaching I have used "gimmicks" to get teams to play hard. There were a couple times I even stretched the truth to get our team to play hard. I remember one year we were playing against a team that we had very little chance of beating and I told the team that the first time we played them that when the players came over to shake my hand when they were introduced before the game, that they all said that they were going to "kick our ass." That wasn't actually the truth. My team was so fired up that we almost had a fight before the "tip off." We played so hard that night that we lost by a couple of points to a team we should not have come within 20 points of. I don't recommend lying to your team, but I felt it was a desperate situation and if we didn't do something we were going to get embarrassed. So gimmicks can work, but you can't rely on a steady dose of them.

Another idea that I used to get players to play hard was to copy what the U.S. military teaches and believes. It is my understanding that combat soldiers are taught to fight for each other, that their loyalty to each other will motivate them to "go the limit" in fighting the enemy. We constantly talked about this theory to the team and put them in several exercises to try to develop that type of attitude. And we would always mention to the players not to let their teammates down.

## Characteristics of a Team Playing Hard

1. Running the floor on offense—fast break.
2. Running hard back on defense.
3. Diving for loose balls.
4. Taking charges.
5. Closing out on shooters.
6. Fighting through screens—off or on ball.
7. Not allowing yourself to be screened.
8. Saving balls going out of bounds.
9. Getting to the offensive boards.
10. Overall team defense.

Coach Bob Huggins of West Virginia in speaking at a recent coaches clinic, indicated that he was thinking about his dog one day and how he was going to train it to go fetch a stick and teach it how to sit. He said it dawned on him that training that dog is similar to how he gets his players to "play hard." *Run - Sit.* If a player doesn't play hard you *Run* him and if he still doesn't play hard then you *Sit* him. This system must work because Huggins teams play as hard as any in the country.

In conclusion, there are many ways that coaches can get their players to play hard. What works for one coach may not work for another. But I believe the bottom line is that the coach must expect his/her team to play hard, develop it in his/her culture, and simply not put up with lazy play.

"A guy who gives you less than what he has to give is, one, telling you what he thinks of you, and two, telling you what he thinks of himself." —Pete Carrill

# 16 The Story of Brian Kelly (Never Give Up On Your Dreams)

During the summer of 1990, while I was the head basketball coach at Cincinnati State College, I met an extraordinary young man by the name of Brian Kelly at one of our open gyms. Brian at the time was a freshmen at the University of Cincinnati. He was about 6 foot 6 inches tall and was built like a football player. He certainly passed the eye test as a basketball player. He drew my attention just on his looks.

He asked if he could get in some "run" and I told him that he was free to play as much as he liked. Before he started playing, I asked him a few questions, one being where he played high school ball? He told me that he had never played any high school basketball, that he had been cut every year. Of course, that answer didn't quite match his physical status. "How could a guy that size not play high school basketball?"

I watched him closely as he ran up and down the floor in our open gym. He didn't do anything good or bad, he was just out there. But there was something about him, a confidence about him, a self-assuredness, and a presence that you had to take a second look.

Brian, was also a talker and a tremendous salesman. He was Mr. Personality—Plus. In a matter of minutes he knew everyone in the gym, and was carrying on conversations, and giving out encouragement to them. I could see that he had leadership potential.

He came to every open gym that summer and continually asked me to give him a scholarship to play basketball for our college. I repeatedly put him off. I just wasn't sure about him as a player. He really never did anything in open gym where I thought that he could play for us. As I said earlier, he was a good salesman, and he continued to work on me all summer. He had such a great attitude and I could see how much he loved the game and enjoyed playing that I was starting to warm to his interest in playing for us. The more I was around him, the more I appreciated what he was selling. And believe me, he was always selling.

A week before school was going to start, I called him and told him that I was offering him our scholarship, which wasn't anything more than a few hundred dollars. He was satisfied and rushed to the office to sign the letter-of-intent. He had sold me that "aluminum siding" he was trying to sell me all summer.

His freshmen season started and Brian was anchored to the bench. He wasn't getting much playing time, but I could see that there were some things that he was very good at doing. But he was a very poor shooter, and I gave him a rule that he was not to shoot any further out than 10 feet from the basket. He argued with me, telling me that he was a tremendous shooter, but he abided by my rule. However, I was beginning to see some things, that he was a great team player, always boxed out, a great post defender, took charges, set hard screens, aggressive and always passed the ball to the open man and kept our offense moving. He was starting to get my attention each day in practice.

I had a power forward playing in front of Brian who had signed a scholarship early at Central Michigan University and he was not playing well. Our record at that time was about .500 and I decided to put Brian in the starting line-up. We never lost again until the regional finals. And we beat Vincennes University, our biggest rival, twice that year with Brian in the line-up. Brian did all the "little things" to help us win. His leadership ability in many instances got us over the hump, especially in not letting the team quit. He got into the habit that after practice and after he had eaten dinner he would start calling players to talk to them about practice or about the next game. It was all positive stuff and helped so much with the attitude of the team.

Brian's second year was pretty much a duplicate of the first. There was some improvement but he just kept doing the things that helped us win. We had an outstanding year, 28–5, we beat Vincennes University again twice that year, and were ranked in the top 20 of the NJCAA. We lost one of our outstanding players who was averaging 20 points per game and 10 rebounds per game and we got upset in the regional tournament.

There were no All-American or All-Region or All-League awards for Brian Kelly. But he was probably our MVP. He only averaged 6 points per game, and 6 rebounds per game for his combined two years.

When the season was over, Brian came into my office and we talked about the season and what he wanted to do in the future. He had a couple of Division III and a couple of NAIA schools that were recruiting him. During the season, a coach from a Mid American Conference school came in and watched Brian practice, but we never heard from him again. Brian expressed to me that he wanted to play Division I basketball. I told him no Division I schools were recruiting him. We had four other players that were being recruited by DI's, but not Brian. I tried to be as positive as I could with him, but basically told him I just didn't think it was going to happen. Brian wouldn't listen to that, he just wouldn't take no for an answer. So he asked me what he could do…and that's were the story really begins.

When he asked me what he could do, I was dumbfounded. I didn't know what to say, I didn't want to completely close the door to Division I. So I just threw out something. I said, "Why don't you send out a letter?" Well, he did just that. He sent out over 300 letters to Division I head coaches, along with what he called his "Basketball Resume." It took him a couple of weeks, but he got them all sent out.

Well, he got answers from six Division I universities. Four of the letters thought he was applying for a job and sent him an application, and two were letters of interest. The two letters of interest were from St. Louis University and Big East member Georgetown University (Hoyas).

The next thing I know, I am getting a call from one of Georgetown's assistant coaches. He starts out by giving me his name and that he is calling from Georgetown University and not the Georgetown from Kentucky. We talked about Brian for a while and then he said that Coach John Thompson would be calling me in a couple of days to talk about Brian, that he was very interested in Brian.

Coach Thompson called and we talked more about Brian and he asked me to send up some video tape on him. One thing Coach

Thompson said was that he was impressed that Brian was the student government president. I told Coach Thompson the truth about Brian, about his leadership ability and how he was such a team player. But that he only averaged 6 points and 6 rebounds per game. I sent the tape and within a couple of days Coach Thompson called back and said that he would like for Brian to visit, and that he would be sending the airline ticket.

The next conversation I had with Brian was about what he was going to wear to the visit. We must have talked for over an hour about his wardrobe. Brian talked about if he dressed up (coat and tie) that they would think he was a "square," and if he dressed too casual they might think he wasn't cut out for that level of university. So it was a dilemma, but after much discussion we went with the coat and tie.

One of the things that has always amazed me is that Coach Thompson saw what Brian Kelly's assets were when other coaches completely missed on what he could do for their team. But I can see how if they just looked at his statistics they might not have an interest.

Brian visited Georgetown for two days and without saying, Coach Thompson fell in love with him. He kept asking Brian if he was for real. At breakfast on Sunday morning, Coach Thompson offered Brian a full athletic scholarship to play basketball at Georgetown University. Coach Thompson drove Brian to the airport to come back to Cincinnati. After Brian was on the plane, Coach Thompson came onto the plane and told the pilot that Brian had just signed to play for Georgetown. So after the pilot got the plane above the clouds, the pilot came on the intercom and told the passengers that they had a celebrity on board, that Brian Kelly had just signed to play basketball for Georgetown University. The passengers erupted in applause.

The applause was fitting for a young man who had just taken victory out of the jaws of defeat and achieved his most coveted "dream." Who would have thought it!?

Brian graduated from Georgetown University with a business degree and met his future wife. They moved to California were she became an ER doctor and Brian got his law degree from Pepperdine University. He would later work for Robert Shapiro who was a lawyer in the OJ Simpson case.

I ran into Coach Thompson at a Final Four a few years ago and we talked about Brian. He said, "Brian is one of my favorite players of all-time."

Brian Kelly, #40.

# 17 Rory's Glory (Best Player I Ever Coached)

In the summer of 1979, I received a call from then head basketball coach, Bob Staak, of Xavier University. He wanted to know if I would be interested in a player who had signed at St. John's University by Coach Lou Carnesecca. The player's name was Rory Glasco, a 6' 4" forward from Hempstead, New York, and West Babylon High School. Things were not working out at St. John's and Rory was looking to go to a junior college. Of course I told Coach Staak that I would be interested.

So I called Rory and talked with him and then talked with his mother. Rory and his mother were interested, mainly because Rory had an uncle who lived in Cincinnati. It was a stroke of good *ole luck* which sometimes happens in recruiting.

The next day, Rory was sitting in my office at 9:00 a.m. He had taken an early flight from New York, needless to say he was excited to have this second chance to play college basketball.

In the meantime, I called Coach Carnesecca to see what he had to say about Rory. He had nothing but compliments about Rory's playing ability, and even stated that he thought he could play in the NBA. But he wasn't too happy that Rory wasn't going to be playing for the Red Storm.

Our basketball program at Cincinnati Technical College (now called Cincinnati State) was just three years into its existence. The program didn't have a lot of respect at the time and we just hadn't been in the business long enough to be taken seriously. That all changed with the emergence of Rory Glasco.

When Rory walked between those lines he was all about basketball. I never saw a kid love to play the game as much as Rory did. He always played hard and was the ultimate team player. He was very unselfish and was as intelligent about the game as any player that I ever saw. But when he left the confines of the basketball court he was this playful, charismatic jokester, who mainly wanted to entertain people and establish his good guy persona.

Rory had nicknames for all of the players, and he was a genius at picking out these names. He named one of our players "Charles Manson," another one "Plate" because he said he had a plate in his head, another player he called "First Man" because he looked like the first man on earth, and then there was "Mule," because our bus hit a mule coming back from a game and Rory said this player looked like the Mule. None of the players ever got mad at Rory for these names, they would just laugh and laugh as he would explain the names he had given everyone.

Rory was a 6' 4" small forward, who was quick, strong, instinctive, versatile player with "hops," whose best shot was usually a missed shot because he was so relentless on the offensive boards, he would snag the missed shot and convert it for two points. He was poetry in motion, he had such a flow to his game and was just such a joy to watch play that we were getting people off the streets to come and watch him play. A local sportswriter labeled Rory as the best college basketball player in Cincinnati, including the University of Cincinnati and Xavier.

His freshmen year he averaged 17.6 points per game, 11.2 rebounds, and 4.8 assists. During the two years he played we had back to back 27–6 records. Rory's freshmen year we had to play him at center, because we were so small as a team. Needless to say Rory was becoming the cornerstone of our newly organized basketball program.

Rory's sophomore season was a banner year for both Rory and our basketball program. As stated before, we recorded another 27–6 record and beat Vincennes University in the Regional XII NJCAA Tournament. We had never beaten Vincennes and our players celebrated way too much and exerted way too much energy and we got upset the next day by Sinclair.

Rory averaged 27.6 points per game, 14.5 rebounds per game, and 4 assists per game. He was named as a National Junior College Athletic Association Division I, "All-American." Cincinnati Tech (Cincinnati State) was ranked in the top ten of the NJCAA Division I rankings most of the year. We were finally on the JUCO map as a legit program and a program that was going to have to be dealt with.

Rory Glasco still holds every record in men's basketball at Cincinnati State. There is a very good chance that none of his records will ever be broken. His records include:

Most career points (1406)

Most points in a single season (822)

Most career rebounds (810)

Most rebounds in a single season (440)

Rory Glasco

Most career assists (416)

Most assists in a single season (258)

Most field goals (600)

Most rebounds in a single game (26)

During Glasco's sophomore season he was recruited heavily. At least one university from every major conference came in to see Rory play and talk with him. Many of these coaches became constant visitors to our campus. Several of them were there on a weekly basis. I remember Darrell Hedric at Miami University (Ohio) chasing Rory down the hallway, and Rollie Massimino from Villanova being on campus so much, you would have thought he was a member of the faculty. Then there was Randy Vernon from Cumberland College, an NAIA school, who we had to get another chair in my office, for he hung around so much, hoping that Rory might slide down to his level. All of that effort eventually paid off for Coach Vernon. Virginia Tech's assistant coaches attended just about every one of our home games. It was a constant bombardment of college coaches from all over the country. Our program was starting to cross over from Off-Broadway to Broadway with all the excitement surrounding Rory.

Out of all the coaches that came to campus to recruit Rory, Coach Bill Hodges from Indiana State and his assistants were there just about on a daily basis. Of course Bill Hodges coached Larry Bird when they had their famous run in the NCAA tournament and the classic game against Michigan State and a fellow named Magic Johnson. If you are a basketball fan you know that rivalry between Bird and Magic continued a long time in the NBA.

I could tell that Rory was starting to lean toward Indiana State. They had told him that they might Red Shirt him and that seemed to interest Rory. There was no question that Indiana State was going to commit to Rory and that they believed that Rory had some of the same basketball abilities that their best player ever Larry Bird had. Believe me Rory was a similar player to Bird, not quite in that range, but close. Rory had the same passing abilities that Bird possessed. Rory could do the look away passes, and over the shoulder type passes that Bird could do. Rory was not as good a shooter, but made up for it by his tenuous offensive rebounding. Rory was not Larry Bird, but there were some similarities in their games.

Rory decided to attend Indiana State and they indeed Red Shirted him, which was to Rory's liking. Things were going very well at Indiana State for Rory until the university decided to let Coach Hodges go. Rory called me at 2:00 a.m. in a panic and told me what had happened to Coach Hodges. No one could believe that with all the success he had and being the coach of Larry Bird that they would part ways with him, but they did. Rory wanted to transfer. He was very loyal to Coach Hodges and he didn't want to play for anyone else. Rory also told me that he was tired of sitting out and he wanted to play right away. The only place he could transfer would be an NAIA school because of the transfer rules. So he wanted me to call Coach Randy Vernon at Cumberland College. It was coming true that all the time that Coach Vernon put in recruiting Rory was finally paying off for him.

Rory transferred to Cumberland College and played for the Patriots for one year. He averaged 18.2 points and 11 rebounds per game. Cumberland College recorded the best record in school's history at 33–3, which still stands to this day. They also made the NAIA National Tournament.

After the season was over at Cumberland, Rory moved back to Hempstead, New York. Rory is a legend to all those who played with him, and all those who got the opportunity to watch him play. Ironically, when I tell someone that I was the Coach at Cincinnati Tech (Cincinnati State), the first thing they will say is Rory Glasco.

I think a lot about the years I spent in coaching, the good times, the bad times, the many players I had the privilege of coaching and the time that we spent together. The two years I spent with Rory Glasco were special, and I believe the players that played with him feel the same way. It was luck and circumstance that brought us all together with Rory. It was a magic moment that went by all too quickly.

I wanted to put this story about Rory Glasco in this book because I believe coaches can learn something from the story. Coaching extraordinary talent is different. I don't believe you can treat this type of player the same as the other players, not that you favor them over the other players, but that you have to understand that the game comes naturally to them, they do things with such ease. This type of talent can't be taught. I think you can improve this type of player, but that natural ability is just there. They require little coaching compared to the other players. One of the things that I tried to instill in Rory was that he needed to try to make others better, and that he did. The other thing that I did with Rory was to challenge him in many ways, and to make sure that he stayed focused. So I played him at different positions at times, or matched him up on defense with the other teams best player on offense, or set game goals like pulling down a certain number of rebounds.

I hope that you get an opportunity to coach the extraordinary talented player, no matter what level you are coaching. I feel that I am so fortunate to have had that experience. Many coaches coach their whole careers and never have the opportunity to do this. If you do have the opportunity, adjust your coaching, and savor every minute of the experience.

"You better be on the same page as your star player. If not, you're going to be in trouble." —David Blatt, past coach of the Cleveland Cavaliers

*Rory Glasco's statistics provided by Cincinnati State and Cumberland College.

# 18 Coaching Special Situations

Every basketball coach from youth basketball all the way to the NBA has to be prepared for situations that occur anytime during the game, but particularly late in games. Games can be lost if the coach is not prepared to know what to do or have a play prepared in these late game situations. These special situations occur in the game of basketball, no matter what level you are coaching.

As mentioned in other chapters, the youth coach and sometimes junior high or even high school coaches don't have a lot of practice time. So working on special situations is very difficult and must be put on a priority list. But if you can find a few minutes at the end of practice to work on special situations your team will be much more prepared.

The internet is loaded with information on special and late game situations. You can find any situation that you need information on. I always had one of my assistant coaches keep a notebook on the bench of special and late game situation plays, so that we could quickly review it with the team at a time out.

Things that are most often covered as special situations are as follows:

1. Late game situations where score, time, and fouls are involved.

2. Out of bounds plays, with little time left on the clock. Under-Side-Deep Corner.

3. Choosing late game defense, usually switching man-to-man is used at half court.

4. "Home run" set plays for last second desperation situations.

5. "Get the ball to half court," play and call time out, if enough time.

6. Special press breaker, to get the ball inbounds. Under opponents basket or sideline.

7. Fouling situations. Do you have a foul to give? Who do you want to shoot your free throws—get the ball in their hands. How and when to foul.

8. Tip out plays on free throws.

9. What to do if you are up by 3 points, with less than 9 seconds to go. Do you foul?

10. Playing through "bad calls."

11. Set plays to get a shot with little time remaining.

12. 2 for 1 situations. When there is enough time in the half to shoot—get a defensive stop—get a second shot before the half ends.

13. When do you shoot at the end of the game, when score is tied? Six seconds has been my preferred time, so you have time to get a tip in or offensive rebound.

14. Out of bounds defense, under opponents basket or sideline.

15. Time outs—it's always a good idea to save at least one.

16. Tip play for jump ball at start of overtime game. (If you have height or jumping advantage.)

17. Quick hitting plays.

18. Free throw plays to get rebound when you are shooting the free throw.

19. When to put a player back into the game with 4 fouls. It's better to put them in too early rather than too late, in my opinion.

20. Calling a time out after your team scores is good strategy.

## Other Notes

1. Play game Down 8–3 minutes to go and Up 8–3 minutes to go.

2. Practice last-second and half court shots in practice.

3. Keep a notebook of special situations and plays on the bench.

4. Have your team captains involved in late game situations in practice. Have them coach the team for the special situations.

5. In late game situations, keep in mind that the offensive fundamentals of timing, spacing, and execution is your best bet.

6. Of course, you want to get the ball to your best shooter at the end of games.

7. Get the most out of your time-outs, late in games.

8. Time management, when to slow up or speed up game.

9. Be cool under pressure and don't let the situation change your demeanor.

Fran Fraschilla 3 C's of coaching in pressure situations:

1. Clear

2. Concise

3. Confident

I have included after this chapter a "Special Situations Planning Chart." This chart was devised by Coach Brian Williams and is part of the information on special situations at www.coachingtoolbox.net.

"Be there before you get there." —Brad Stevens, Boston Celtics

"Notoriety of a coach is proportional to team's ability to execute under pressure." —Hubie Brown

"You learn so much from seeing what other coaches do, what other teams do, what some of the great players do instinctually." —Shaka Smart, University of Texas

# Special Situations Planning Chart

| Possible Starting Points for the Situation | Home Score | Time Remaining | Possession Arrow | Guest Defense | Home Fouls |
|---|---|---|---|---|---|
| You score a basket with the clock running | +5 | 2:00 | Home | Packing Man to Man | 3 |
| Your opponent scores a basket with the clock running | +4 | 1:00 | Visitor | 2-3 zone | 4 |
| You make a second of two (or third of three) free throws | +3 | :25 | | 3-2 zone | 5 |
| Converting to defense when your player misses the final free throw | +2 | :15 | | Pressure Man to Man | 6 |
| Underneath your basket inbounding | +1 | :10 | | Switching Defenses | 7 |
| Sideline Inbounds on your offensive end | Tied | :08 | | | 8 |
| Your ball going the full length of the court | -1 | :05 | | No Full Court Press | 9 |
| Opponent inbounding underneath their basket | -2 | :03 | | Man to Man Full Court Press | 10 |
| Opponent sideline inbounds | -3 | :02 | | Zone Full Court Press Alignment | |
| Opponent ball going full length of court | -4 | :01 | | | |
| Other | -5 | | | Half Court Trap | |

Circle one from each column and you can quickly come up with an end of game situation to rehearse at the end of each night's practice. You can insert your own ideas in any of the blank boxes.

Chart from www.coachingtoolbox.net.

| Visitor Fouls | Home Timeouts Left | Visitor Timeouts Left | Players in Foul Trouble | Special Rules/Notes |
|---|---|---|---|---|
| 3 | 0 | 0 | | Designate a 2nd team player's free throws as automatic. If he or she is fouled, the second team gets 2 points if in bonus. |
| 4 | 1 | 1 | | Make an obvious bad call against the 1st (home) team to simulate how to handle a bad call in a game. |
| 5 | 2 | 2 | | Designate a 2nd team player as "making" every shot he or she can get off to simulate playing against a great scorer. |
| 6 | 3 | 3 | | Don't call fouls on 2nd team—within reason to teach 1st team to be strong with the ball at the end of the game with lead |
| 7 | 4 | 4 | | Devise your own special rules that make practice more challenging for your first team |
| 8 | 5 | 5 | | |
| 9 | | | | |
| 10 | | | | |
| | | | | |
| | | | | |
| | | | | |

# 19 Coaching Youth Basketball

According to several definitions of the word youth that I have read; youth is explained to take place between four years old and sixteen or eighteen years old, when maturity takes place. However, for our purposes, I believe youth basketball is up to the age of eleven. I believe at the age of eleven, players are able to go to the next step of receiving coaching, and should no longer be considered youth basketball.

First of all, the youth coach has an obligation and responsibility to teach the fundamentals of the game and to teach teamwork to his or her team. You have a very important job!

According to @BreakthruBball, there are three very important concepts you need to consider:

"1. Kids need to be highly active! Keep them moving and not standing in lines and keep the ball in their hands as much as possible.

2. Kids want to feel successful! Make sure the players have developed their skills before adding pressure and competition.

3. Kids want to have lots of fun! This is an important stage for young players and your actions could determine whether they enjoy sports or not."

# Type of Offense

I believe that using a very simplified motion offense is the answer for youth basketball. It should be the same as my recommended system offense, but more simplistic with regard to rules and actions that you designate. I like the motion offense for youth basketball because it teaches both player and ball movement. But teaching this offense should not deter you from spending the majority of your time teaching fundamentals. I would recommend using a 5-out motion offense, with no designated post. I also recommend my teaching system for the motion offense in that you first introduce the open post offense to get players used to cutting and screening in an organized manner. Then follow up with teaching the "2-Rule Motion Offense." (See Chapter 22)

Always keep in mind that a good percentage of your points are going to be scored in "Unstructured Play" as I described in Chapter 12.

As I have mentioned several times in this book, teaching spacing on offense is a priority, and especially with the youth basketball team. Here is a list of the things that you should be teaching on offense:

*Offensive Fundamentals That Should Be Taught*

1. Teach squaring up to the basket and the triple threat position. Triple threat is catching the ball and squaring up to the basket so you can either shoot, pass, or dribble.

2. Teach V Cuts and getting open to receive the pass.

3. Teach Cutting—Pass and cut a good drill to use.
4. Teach screening away.
5. Introduce reading screens.
6. Teach passing away from the defense.
7. Move the ball from side-top-side.
8. Spacing—15 to 18 foot distance.

## Break The Game Down

I think it is important at the youth basketball level to play a lot of 1 on 1, 2 on 2, and 3 on 3 basketball. There could be a case made that 5 on 5 basketball should not start until the age of 10 or later. In the 3 on 3 game, there is more space and the players get to touch the ball more often. I believe they have a better chance of learning the game the right way. Certainly it is important to incorporate 1 on 1, 2 on 2, and 3 on 3 in your practices.

## Youth Basketball Defense

For youth basketball I think it is mandatory that you play man-to-man (girl-to-girl) defense. It will be very *wild* at the beginning, but the young player will begin to pick up the defense after a few games. The major problem that you will have with the man-to-man defense will be players finding their man (girl) coming back on defense.

Having the players talk and communicate to everyone who they are guarding will help solve that problem.

Most youth programs don't allow pressing and some don't allow stealing the ball from the dribbler.

Usually there is not enough practice time in youth basketball to really teach man-to-man defense correctly, but you may be able to start teaching the fundamentals.

Jonah Gregg, my grandson, six years old.

## Defensive Fundamentals That Should Be Taught

1. Defensive stance.
2. Defensive slides.
3. Knowing where the ball is and getting "Help Side."
4. Boxing out.
5. Finding your man or girl and picking them up.
6. Ball-you-man concept.
7. Seeing ball and man (Pointing to ball and man).

## Other Ideas

1. Don't over coach and try to correct every defensive mistake.

2. Teach sportsmanship.

3. Build confidence.

4. Teach how to play, not learning plays.

5. Do not get involved in getting on the referees, focus on your team.

6. Make sure your kids pay attention—tell them to look at you when you are speaking.

7. Don't correct every mistake the youth player makes.

8. Don't be concerned about winning.

9. Teach the big kids how to dribble, pass, and shoot (not just stand under the basket).

## Teaching Young Players How to Shoot Lay Ups

Teaching the youth player how to properly shoot lay ups, from both the right and left side of the basket, is a major task for the youth coach, particularly at the younger levels.

A tip on teaching this fundamental is to take the dribble out of the equation. It is easier for the young player to just focus on the one fundamental of shooting the lay up and not the dribbling. I have found this to work very well in teaching the lay up to young players. If they have their strong side hand lay up perfected, but need work on the off hand this drill works very well.

## Teaching Young Players How To Dribble

I like to start teaching dribbling using two basketballs. This forces the young player to use both his dominant and weak hand. They start by being stationary and dribbling the two basketballs simultaneously, both basketballs hitting the floor at the same time. Then we dribble, alternating each ball hitting the floor. We do this for a period of 5 to 7 minutes.

John Hurley, my son, top left, and Jessica Hurley, my granddaughter, front row, second from the right.

The next progression is to zig zag the ball going at about half speed, first having the basketballs hit the floor simultaneously and then alternating. Again, we do this for 5 to 7 minutes.

I believe there are four types of dribbling that need to be mastered. They are:

1. Speed dribble—right and left hand.
2. Reverse or spin dribble.
3. Crossover—keep ball below knees on crossover.
4. Behind the back.

I also recommend using "dribble glasses." It forces the young player not to look at the ball when dribbling. These may be purchased online at Korney Board Aids, www.kbacoach.com.

## National Youth Sports Coaches Association (NYSCA)

The NYSCA is a part of the National Alliance of Youth Sports. This organization has two training programs for youth coaches. One is the general coaches training program that covers topics coaches of all sports need to know, such as working with parents, motivating kids, building confidence, instilling good sportsmanship, safety, and nutrition and hydration, among many other areas.

In the sport-specific training, coaches learn how to teach the basic skills and fundamentals of the particular sport they are coaching, as well as effective drills to use during their practices.

I highly recommend belonging to this organization if you are a youth coach and going through their training programs. They have trained over 3 million coaches since they started in 1981.

Also, these coaching programs are offered on-site in more than 3,000 communities nationwide. Having their certification is a definite plus if you are going to be coaching youth sports.

Jennifer Hurley, my granddaughter.

"The youth coach should be teaching the skills of the game, not how to win games." —Stan Van Gundy

# 20 Daddy Ball

According to PlayKidsSports.com, *Daddy Ball* is a term that has been used to describe when your child's coach has a son or daughter on the same team, and that parent/coach gives their own child more opportunities, playing time, and usually the most popular position on the team.

I think it is wonderful for a dad or a mom to take the opportunity to coach their son or daughter. It is such a great experience to be able to spend time with your child in a sports setting. Having that time with your child during practices and games can't be replaced. I have known many coaches at the high school or college level who have said that it was the greatest experience of their life. Many times it builds an even greater bond between the parent and the child.

I have mentioned youth sports in a couple of other chapters, but I felt that this subject needed to have a chapter all its own.

In an article entitled, "Daddy Ball: The Painful Reality of Youth Sports," by Greg Baumgartner, he states that, "Daddy Ball also serves to cheat the team, because when boys are not played where they fall athletically, the team will be less competitive and the boys will be less motivated. Resulting in a team that is not all it could have been."

I have witnessed *Daddy Ball* many times, but I got a good close up look at it when my six-year-old grandson started playing sports. He played on a basketball team where the coach had his son on the team and to make it worse the coach's best friend was an assistant coach and his son was on the team. I saw my grandson practice and play games, and it was disgusting the favoritism and the selfishness of the coaches. What kept going through my mind was that they were going to ruin my grandson's desire from ever playing basketball.

The coach's son was the point guard and he brought the ball up the floor and the only person he would pass to was the coach's best friend's kid. Other kids on the team would be wide open and they would not pass them the ball. This took place in practice as well as the games. I had a very difficult time watching it. Even on a sideline out of bounds, the coach yelled at his son to not pass my grandson the ball. The coaches did take their sons out of the game, because the rules dictated it.

I think as a parent experiencing *Daddy Ball*, you must be very careful not to make the situation an excuse for your son or daughter. I don't know how many parents I have talked to over the years that have horror stories about *Daddy Ball*. And when I recruited high school players, I would sometimes hear about the Booster Club influencing who the coach played. I think it could become an excuse at every level. College players sometimes have *Scholarship Ball* when one player is getting more scholarship money than another. Even at the pro level, I have heard people say that a player doesn't deserve to play as much, but they play him because he has a *Big Contract*. Maybe it's something you can never get away from.

So, as a parent or player what should you do? Constanza Ulloa-Colina, in her article "How to Deal With Daddy Ball," suggests the following:

> "Stop focusing on the politics or negative aspects of your team and focus on making yourself so good they won't be able to ignore you. If in any instance you are clearly the better athlete on the team and your coach is still playing favorites then just approach him about the issue. A coach will respect you and your concerns much more if you communicate with him or her rather then badmouthing them behind their back, or causing a scene. That advice goes for both players and parents."

University of Louisiana head baseball coach, Tony Robichaux explains what to do if you are on a team with *Daddy Ball*:

> "We tell them all the time, you've got to work while you wait. Most people, in their personal life, they stop working until the door opens, and then they want to work again now that the door is open. But in this profession you've got to work while you wait."

Many parents put up with *Daddy Ball* and say nothing, hoping that they can find a team for their child next year where the coach doesn't have a son or daughter on the team. Sometimes the parent decides to coach a team themselves and reverse the situation. There is no question, it is a frustrating dilemma.

Most *Daddy Ball* coaches don't realize what they are doing or they are in denial about it. They have a very difficult time in honestly evaluating their child's athletic ability. In order to highlight their child they will sacrifice the experience, learning, and progress of the other players on the team.

My suggestion to parents that are coaching their own child is to hold a meeting and tell the players and the player's parents that they are going to be honest about the situation. The *Daddy Coach* should explain that their son or daughter is naturally their favorite player, simply because it is their child. But that he or she will make every effort to be fair and give all players an opportunity. I believe it is very healthy to bring up the situation and discuss it with the players and their parents.

Coach Jon, in his article, "Daddy Ball: What It Is And How To Avoid It" describes the *Daddy Ball* phenomenon this way:

> "This all comes down to control. The coach is in a position of control and therefore determines the fate of all of the players on the team. The parents have no control, and this is an uncomfortable and potentially explosive situation when the lack of control results in unfair treatment—real or perceived."

I sympathize with both sides and having two children I understand how this situation can happen. Here are some things that both the coach and the parents should try to understand:

1. If the coach's kid is simply the team's best player, the other parents need to recognize it and acknowledge it.

2. If the coach's kid is inferior in talent, the coach needs to recognize it.

3. The coach should make decisions as a coach, not a parent.

4. Understand that every parent has a bias about their child.

5. Suggest that the coach use statistics to help determine playing time.

6. The coach and parents should strive to make the team experience a positive, memorable, and fun situation for their child.

7. The coach should think about other means of recognition for the team members, such as giving the game ball or awarding a milk shake to those who perform well.

8. It is important for the coach and parents to promote the idea of accomplishment, such as striving to win the championship. Not just giving everybody a trophy at the end of the season, even if the team had a losing record.

In conclusion, *Daddy Ball* is a very complex problem. I think in many ways open communication between the coach and the parents can be the answer. On both sides of the issue we must understand that what we are fighting is human frailty. It is very difficult to overcome this particular human frailty, but if we bring it out in the open and discuss it at all levels, we have a chance of making it better. I believe that the league organizers or leaders have a responsibility to discuss *Daddy Ball* with their coaches. They might even put some type of guidelines in a manual given to all coaches. I do think we are making progress on this problem, there are more discussions and more articles written on this subject. Even college coaches are beginning to talk about it. What we should all do is make sure that kids don't miss out on any chance to have a wonderful experience and to remember that experience for a lifetime.

"In my opinion, the word 'daddy ball' should never be communicated by the parents to the player." —Amanda Scarborough

# 21 Treating Injuries

Depending at what level you are coaching you may or may not have the services of an Athletic Trainer. Many junior high and high schools have either a full-time trainer or at least a part-time trainer on board. Other youth teams are usually not awarded this type of privilege. Whether you have a trainer or not, however, the responsibility of dealing with injuries rests with the coach.

According to the University of Wisconsin Health and Sports Medicine, "There are an estimated 21.5 million kids between ages 6 and 17 playing competitive youth sports in America. And consequently, it is the most common cause of injuries in kids. It is estimated that 2.7 million kids under age 20 were treated for sports injuries between 2001 and 2009."

When I coached the eighth grade boys basketball team I had to be involved in an Ohio High School Athletic Association coaches certification program. I had to take a first aid class, a CPR class, a coaching class, and pass a test on concussions before I was allowed to coach. In other youth programs such as AAU there are no such requirements. But my recommendation is that you take it upon yourself to be trained in those areas mentioned above.

Here is a list of four common injuries for basketball players:

*Sever's Disease (Heel Pain)*

Sever's disease is inflammation of the growth plate of the heel bone in children. It is provoked by running and jumping and repetitive stress. Treatment for Sever's disease is rest and ice. Once the growth plate fuses, this is no longer a problem. It is fairly common in children.

*Ankle Sprains*

Ankle sprains are among the most common injuries experienced by basketball players. Ankle sprains normally don't require surgery unless they are recurrent. The rehabilitation time needed to return to basketball can vary from 2–8 weeks following the sprain. Treatment includes rest, ice, compression, and elevation, also referred to as R-I-C-E. Wearing ankle braces may prevent serious ankle sprains.

*Anterior Cruciate Ligament (ACL) Injury and Tears*

Anterior Cruciate Ligament (ACL) tears are less common but more severe. In most cases these injuries will require surgery. Proper training can help reduce the likelihood of an ACL tear occurring. Athletes can reduce their risk of ACL injuries by performing training drills that require balance, power, and agility. Adding exercises, such as jumping and balance drills, help improve muscular conditioning and ultimately show a decrease in the risk of ACL injury. Interestingly enough, it appears that females are more susceptible to ACL injury.

*Concussions*

Injuries from concussion have been thought of as football injuries, but they happen in basketball, more so in females. Some studies report that female players experience concussions 240 percent more often than male players. No one really knows why yet.

Dr. Richard Okragly, the director of Bethesda Family Medicine Primary Care and Sports Medicine, indicates that, "it's challenging diagnosing a child or patient with a concussion, based on the vagueness of the symptoms. We are probably erring on the side of caution, as we should, especially with our younger, grade school athletes."

Dr. Okragly lists the common concussion symptoms:

"1. Dizziness

2. Changes in behavior

3. Headaches that aren't normal for the individual

4. Nausea or vomiting

5. Blurred vision

6. Difficulty concentrating

7. Confusion

8. Sensitivity to light"

Other Points:

1. It's important to note, however, that symptoms can take 24 to 48 hours to develop.

2. A majority of people who have sustained a concussion will need to be sidelined for at least 7 to 10 days. Some could take several weeks to heal.

3. If you think a player has experienced a concussion, you have to rely on him or her to let you know that he or she feels fine, which means honesty is critical.

As a coach, if there is any question that one of your players is injured, do not put them back into the game. The athlete may tell you they are all right, but err on the side of caution, even if the game is on the line. No game is worth the health of a child.

If the parent is at the game, it is proper procedure to call the parent to the bench to help care for the player. But the parent should not make the decision as to their son or daughter going back into the game. You as coach should make that decision.

Learning as much as you can about athletic injuries should be a high priority when you accept a coaching position. States are going in the right direction requiring certification in athletic injuries before a person is allowed to coach. If you are coaching in an organization that doesn't require certification, then you must take it upon yourself to do your own certification.

Anyone coaching and leading young people must consider "liability" when making decisions concerning the health of a child. A coach should not be paranoid about liability, but it should always be in the back of your mind.

Kidshealth.org suggests that, "Sprained ankles are the most common basketball injuries, but jammed or broken fingers, bruises, bloody or broken noses, and poked eyes are all too common as well. The walls and bleachers and players are bound to collide going after loose balls and rebounds."

No matter what level you are coaching, the bottom line is to conduct the program in a manner that protects, guards, and shields the athlete from injury. However, injuries are going to happen, it is our job to see to it that there is minimal risk. The NCAA explains their approach in the following statement:

"Intercollegiate athletics programs shall be conducted in a manner designed to protect and enhance the physical and educational well-being of student/athletes." —NCAA Division I Manual

"Children First, Winning Second," —York County, Virginia, Basketball Association

# 22 My Recommended System For the New Basketball Coach

If I were a new basketball coach starting out today, I would use the simplified system that I am going to recommend to you in this chapter, if the age of your team is 11 year olds or older. For teams of 11 year olds and younger, I have recommended a Youth Team System. The system for 11 year olds or older is basically the same system that I used when I took my first basketball coaching job, except I would now recommend the "motion offense" instead of the "flex type offense" that was featured in Ed Jucker's book *Cincinnati Power Basketball.* As I have mentioned before, I borrowed a lot of what I learned in the book from Coach Jucker. It worked well for me in the sense of winning. Our record that year was 17–5 and it worked in the sense that I was able to understand what I was teaching the players. This system afforded me the opportunity to coach something that saw both the players and team improve as the season went on.

I have advocated throughout this book that coaches should learn to use the internet to help them with their coaching. The other night I met a young high school reserve basketball coach at a college game. He came over and sat down next to me and said that he would like to pick my brain for a few minutes. We talked about some drills and some of the things that I practiced on a daily basis, and I asked him if he used the internet to help him coach. He said that he did a little by getting a few drills from the internet. I didn't get the impression that he was familiar with all the information that is available on basketball on the internet. Consequently, I haven't used a lot of diagrams in this book because I would like for you to learn how to use the internet for your coaching. Later in this chapter I have listed my systems and where to find them on the internet, hoping that you will get used to using the internet to coach your team. The internet is certainly not the only tool out there to help you coach, but in my estimation it is the best. The following offenses and defenses are what I used in this simplified system and I explain why I chose this particular strategy.

## Motion Offense

When I started coaching, the motion offense had not yet arrived. I used Coach Ed Jucker's flex offense. Bob Knight was coaching at Army, and he was using an offense called "reverse action." It wasn't until he took the head coaching job at Indiana, that he started using the motion offense. It is still debated as to who actually invented the motion offense but Hank Iba at Oklahoma State seems to be the one most historians give the credit. However, Bob Knight did a lot of research on the offense and came up with a little different version than Iba's. With Knight's success at Indiana the offense became very popular and received a lot of notoriety. I recommend this offense to any new coach because it is simple to teach and I believe it is the best offense to teach kids how to play basketball. Also, you can make the offense as simple or as complicated as you want, adjusting it to whatever level you are coaching or the ability of your players.

I believe I have a rather unique method of teaching the motion offense. I first introduce the "open post" offense to my team before I start teaching motion offense. I have found that the open post offense is a great precursor to learning the motion offense. The open post has many of the same rules and actions of the motion offense, it is just a more structured approach, which I believe helps players learn the motion offense. (You can see a great explanation on YouTube of Bob Huggins' Open Post Motion Offense.) I would usually practice the open post for a couple of weeks and then go to a 4 @ 1 motion set (4 perimeter players and 1 post).

Out of the 4 @ 1 set, I would start teaching a very simplified motion offense that I called "2 Rule Motion Offense." I discovered this offense from Sylvia Hatchell, Women's Basketball Coach at North Carolina University. The two rules are as follows:

1. On Guard to Guard Pass—Down screen.
2. On Guard to Wing Pass—Cut and fill.

On the down screen I would teach different cuts off the screen, which incorporated having to read the defense. They are:

1. Pop—Step back off the screen for a shot.
2. Curl—Curl cut to the basket.
3. Backcut—Go behind the screen.
4. Flare Screen—Screen then re-screen.

Depending upon the level you are coaching and the skill level you are coaching you might want to consider adding to the 2 Rule Motion Offense. Dribble hand offs and ball screens can be incorporated into the offense very easily. Of course set plays could be added as well.

Offenses such as Ball Screen and Dribble Drive can be incorporated in the motion offense. The motion offense can be taught in a short period of time and does not require enormous minutes of practice time, thus allowing more practice time to be spent on the fundamentals of the game both offense and defense. It also frees up more practice time to be spent on your team defense.

This offense also allows for teaching of team principles such as shot discipline, team work, and unselfishness.

As mentioned in Chapter 12, unstructured play will account for a good percentage of points that your team is going to score. But, your structured offense is very important in the success of your team.

## Basic Man to Man Defense

Once you learn that the secret to winning basketball games and being successful as a team, is *defense*, then you will have unlocked the key to the entire game of basketball! But selling this concept to your players is no easy task, as I explained in Chapter 11, Motivational Techniques For Teaching Defense. As I have stated several times in this book, I think it is the coach's responsibility and duty to teach man-to-man defense. I don't see any problem with playing some zone defense. But the basic fundamentals of individual and team man-to-man defensive concepts must not be neglected by the coach. I spoke at a basketball clinic a few year's ago on defense. After I was done speaking, a high school coach came up to me and said "Coach, I tried that man-to-man defense one day in practice and it just didn't work." Well, of course it didn't work. Individual and team defense must be practiced every day. There has to be a commitment to it.

I have softened somewhat on my ideas of not playing zone defense. I believe starting with junior high school (seventh and eighth grade), it is permissible to play some zone defense (no more than 20%), in freshmen basketball (no more than 25%), in junior varsity maybe a little more zone defense, (no more than 30%), and high school (coach's decision).

Jim Boeheim who plays the 2-3 zone almost exclusively at Syracuse University, uses pre-season practice to work on man-to-man, individual, and team defense. He feels that it is important for his players to know the fundamentals of playing man-to-man, because so much of the zone defense uses man-to-man principles.

When I first started coaching, I just extended my half court man-to-man defense to full-court. I tried to deny the inbounds pass, and if we didn't steal the ball, then I would just put pressure on the ball up the floor. We would do some trapping. We used the following rules for trapping:

1. Closest two to guys/girls to ball trap.
2. Have two guys/girls as anticipators (looking to steal the ball).
3. One guy/girl protecting the fort (basket).

## Numbered or Designated Fast Break

I basically chose this fast break system because I liked the simplicity and the accountability of the system. The rules were as follows:

1. Point guard or #1 guard always receives outlet pass.
2. #2 guard would always run the right side on the break.
3. #3 guard would always run the left side on the break.
4. #5 center would always post on same side as #1.
5. #4 forward would be trailer opposite #1.

From time to time, I would have one of my players tell me that they couldn't get to their lane because they were on the other side of the floor. I would say to them, "Do you want to play?" "Get there, or we will find someone who will."

This numbered fast break was also my press offense vs. a man-to-man press. When the clock was running, we would get the ball inbounds as quick as possible to our #1 guard, get our lanes filled and go. If we had trouble getting the ball inbounds #2 guard and #3 guard would come back to the ball in their lanes.

## Zone Press Offense

Again, I chose a zone press breaker that was simple and one that would work against all zone press alignments.

Basically, this zone press breaker ended up in a 2-1-2 offense, which I felt could attack most zone presses. We had a few basic principles:

1. Make sure your best ball handler took the ball out.
2. Try to stay away from corners so you won't get trapped.
3. Always have a guard behind the ball for safety.
4. Catch ball and face your basket.
5. Always move to the ball to catch it.
6. Take time—don't panic.

I would always have a special press breaker play to make sure that we could get the ball inbounds at the end of a close game when the opponent was pressing. The play that I liked was running a player out-of-bounds (which is legal) and having the inbounds player pass it to them, then step the inbounds player in or break him/her to middle for return pass. One of the things that we would get on this sometimes is the defensive reaching over or crossing the end-line, which is a technical foul.

## 1-3-1 Zone Offense

I used the 1-3-1 against all types of zones, such as 2-3, 3-2, and even the 1-3-1. Again, I wanted to keep things simple.

Our rules were:

1. Always have one man behind the zone.
2. Always look to dribble penetrate.

3. Always look for skip passes.
4. Attack the middle of the zone.
5. Have feet ready to step into your shot.
6. Offensive rebound.
7. Be patient—usually takes more time to attack zone.
8. Attack the short corner.

I did use a 1-4 across and a low 1-4 to attack against some zone defenses. But these would be quick hitter plays. I liked the 1-4 across, against the 1-3-1 half court trap, especially screening the top man on the 1-3-1. I also had a lot of success using a low 1-4 against match-up zones. I would even throw the ball corner to corner (over top of zone) in low 1-4 offense.

## Out of Bounds Plays

There are hundreds and hundreds of out-of-bounds plays that you can find on the internet. I chose a pick-the-picker play that I liked to run against a man-to-man out-of-bounds defense. I had two out-of-bounds plays that we ran and a couple end of game out-of-bounds plays. You must also have a sideline out-of-bounds play.

I did have a tip-back play that I used when a team zoned our out-of-bounds. It was simple:

1. #3 took it out.
2. #2 was in opposite corner of #3.
3. #1 was at top of key.

4. #4 was on ball side elbow.

5. #5 set up as close to end line on the ball.

When #3 slapped the ball, #4 broke to ball-side corner, and #5 started walking backwards with his hands in the air. #2 would stand in opposite corner and #1 would locate anywhere if #3 needs to throw the ball for safe pass. #3 would lob the ball up in the air to #5 and step inbounds to the edge of the backboard. #5 would then tip the ball to #3 for a lay up.

When I watch high school and college basketball games, I am amazed at how many times I see games lost because a team cannot run an out-of-bounds play. They end up getting a 5 second count or throwing it away. And I can't believe the teams that throw the ball all the way in the back court just to get the ball inbounds.

Out-of-bounds plays are important and practice time needs to be spent on them. But only have a few plays and make them simple.

## 2-3 Zone Defense

As I have emphasized many times in this book, I am a believer in man-to-man defense. However, I do think there is a place in a team's arsenal for some zone defense. The zone defense that I used the most was the Syracuse 2-3 Zone Defense. (And I have given you the web address to learn all about this defense.)

I would use a zone defense for the following reasons:

1. To protect players in foul trouble.
2. To protect a lead at the end of a game.
3. To take advantage of a poor outside shooting team.
4. To neutralize an outstanding guard who can penetrate.

## Half Court Trap Offense

Here are a few rules that we had to attack the half court trap:

1. Attack usually with a 2-1-2 offense.
2. Have two guards pass back and forth before the ball goes over the half court line (make sure one guard is slightly behind other guard). This gets defense shifting.
3. Have continuity in the offense.
4. Always have the players pass the ball opposite from where they received it.

*See Hurley's System on page 189 for recommendations of what a young coach should include in his/her offensive and defensive system.

# 23 Suggestions for the New Coach

Whether you are coaching basketball because you got roped into coaching your son or daughter's team or you were hired to coach basketball from elementary school to high school, you are in for a very difficult time. You want to do things correctly and you want to make sure that the young people you are coaching learn as much as possible. Here are some suggestions and some ideas on getting started.

## Coaching Advice

1. Find a mentor—Most high school and college coaches are open to the idea of letting you attend practices, and this may also allow you to get your foot in the door by asking that coach to be your mentor. Basketball camps in the summer are great places to find a mentor as well. A retired coach may be the perfect mentor for you. The most important thing is to build a relationship with someone before you ask that coach if they will be your mentor.

2. Find an assistant coach—This may be very difficult to do. But, look for someone that will be loyal and would be coaching for all the right reasons.

3. Find the right equipment—You will need at least six (6) basketballs, a dozen orange cones, scrimmage vests, and floor placards (to mark offense and defense positions). Most likely the league or organization will provide most of the things that you will need.

4. Find a team manager/secretary—Again, this may be very difficult to do. Finding someone to collect fees, communicate with team members, and act as equipment manager is crucial.

5. Ask For Help—Sometimes the coaching position can be overwhelming so don't be afraid to ask for help.

## Finding A Mentor (Every Coach Needs A Mentor!)

Of the coaching advice mentioned above, I believe this is the most important one. It is essential that the new coach find someone who can tell him what a coach does, how to discipline players, how to handle the team and individual players, how to handle parents and outside influences, as well as the Xs and Os. Ron Ekker of Basketball Talk Pro has a very good web post on "Learning to Coach From a Mentor." He emphasizes the following points:

"1. Get the right person. Someone higher than you, someone who has been successful.

2. To get a mentor you must build a relationship. This is usually a slow process. You will need patience.

3. Don't just choose a mentor because you like them.

4. Understand that finding a mentor is not an easy task.

5. The best method of finding a mentor is get to know people and learn and listen."

Side note: The Women's Basketball Coaching Association (WBCA) has a mentoring program.

## Oath For Basketball Coaches

It is important to understand the goals of your job as the basketball coach. I believe it is imperative that you follow a guideline similar to the Hippocratic Oath that physicians take when they begin to practice medicine. The following Oath for basketball coaches was developed by the National Youth Sports Safety Foundation:

"1. I acknowledge that children (players) participate to have fun, and the game is for the youth, not adults.

2. I (and my Assistants) will be positive role models for our children (players), and I will encourage good sportsmanship by showing respect and courtesy.

3. I will not encourage any behavior or practices that would be considered unsportsmanlike.

4. I will teach my children (players) to play by the rules and to resolve conflict without resorting to violence and hostility.

5. I will encourage my children (players) to treat other players, coaches, officials and spectators with respect, regardless of race, creed, color, or ability.

6. I will teach my children (players) that doing one's best is more important than winning.

7. I will praise my children (players) for competing fairly.

8. I will never ridicule or yell at my children (players) or others for making a mistake or losing a competition.

9. I will emphasize to my children (players) skill development and practice over winning.

10. I will promote the spiritual, emotional and physical well being of the participants ahead of any personal desire I may have for my children (players) to win."

A footnote: It is important for your team to win. Winning develops many positive traits, but you should not sacrifice teaching about life and developing the skills of basketball. The higher level that you coach, the importance of winning raises.

## Beyond The Xs And Os

1. Know the custodians, the cafeteria servers, the cafeteria cooks, etc. and treat them with respect.

2. Know "Chain of Command" and adhere to its procedures.

3. Communicate with parents before you do anything else.

4. As a coach, expect to be challenged and attacked.

5. If you have been hired to coach, understand that it is im-

portant for the administration to know what is going on with your program. Engage your boss.

6. Understand that you must get along with people outside of the team and build relationships.

7. Play the best players or the players that give you the best chance to win, not the principal's son or daughter or board member's son or daughter. If you are coaching your own child, make sure that you are fair.

8. Seek regular feedback. It's important to know what others think so you can evaluate and make changes if needed.

9. Keep growing and developing, involve yourself in professional development. If you're interested in advancing in the coaching profession, think about an internship or graduate assistant program.

10. Learn the official rules of the game of basketball. The best web site I have found is: www.fiba.com/basketball-rules. Remember the rules for high school, college and the NBA/WNBA are a little different.

11. Be humble and be positive in everything that you do.

Below are some quotes I have collected that stand out to me and might be helpful for you as you are coaching and developing your staff:

"Surround yourself with people you trust. Have people around you who will support your decisions, work hard for you, and help the kids for all the right reasons." —Eric Flannery Head Coach, St. Edward High School

"I would offer this advice to a new coach just starting a career: Build relationships with your players both on and off the court."
—Don Showalter Head Coach, Iowa City High School

"One of the best decisions that I ever made as a head coach was building a very strong, loyal and honest coaching staff."
—Dori Oldaker Head Coach, Mt. Lebanon High School

"Keep the big picture in mind and be yourself."
—Brad Stevens, Boston Celtics

"Either love your players or get out of coaching."
—Bobby Dodd, Georgia Tech

"Coaching is a profession of love."
—Eddie Robinson, Grambling State University

# 24 The Junior High and AAU Experiment

After I retired from coaching basketball, I decided to take a junior high coaching position coaching eighth grade boys basketball. Then a year later I coached a high school girls AAU team. My motivation for accepting these positions was to gain experience coaching at these levels. I thought it would give me a better perspective to help me write this book. I also wanted to give something back to the game and I thought this was a good way to do that. Both coaching situations were the most difficult coaching jobs I have ever had. Some of that difficulty I am sure was caused by the fact that I had never coached at that level. There were many adjustments that I had to make which I will talk about in this chapter. I came out of the experience having a new found appreciation for the coaches that coach at the lower levels.

## Choosing The Players For The Junior High Team

The system that we had at this particular junior high school was a good one in that we had two eighth grade boys team. Seventh and eighth grade boys and girls had two teams each, so, we were able to have somewhere between 20 to 24 players total involved in the program. They were all going to get some game experience and practice every day. It was a great system in my mind because I believe it is very difficult at that age to really know who is going to be the better players. They grow, mature, and develop at different paces.

I have outlined a plan for choosing your team in Chapter 5.

## Choosing The Players For The AAU Girls Team

Choosing the players for the AAU (Amateur Athletic Union) team was entirely different. I didn't have much say on who was going to be on the team. The director of the AAU program, basically selected the players. The players were from many different schools, and of course their parents had to pay a fee for them to play on the team. However, the state athletic rules prohibited more than two players from one school playing on any one team. Some AAU coaches recruit for their teams similarly to the way college coaches recruit.

## Being Too Soft

As a college coach I was pretty hard on my teams, especially on playing defense, rebounding, and playing hard. For whatever reason I didn't feel I could carry that over to the junior high level. I think that was a mistake to some degree. I don't know if I could have demanded as much from them as I did my college teams, but I certainly could have been tougher on them then I was.

I think the key to that problem is that the junior high coach has to find out just what the limit is and I think that is a difficult task. I remember getting on one of my junior high players a little bit and the tears came. That certainly never happened at the college level.

I do think there has to be discipline and the coach must be demanding. Also, the junior high coach must hold the players accountable. There may have to be some experimenting to find that discipline level. My suggestion would be to discuss this with the team and explain to them the necessity of being demanding and holding players accountable. Of course, all coaches have different personalities and without any doubt coaches can be successful with different approaches. But I do believe it is a factor that the new or young coach must address as to how he or she is going to approach discipline with their team.

With the AAU situation, I had never coached girls before and I definitely was way too soft in my approach. However, I enjoyed coaching the girls. I found them to be attentive, more coachable, and more fundamental than the boys.

## System Vs. Non-System

In junior high, the league that we participated is probably one of the toughest leagues in the state of Ohio. I saw a lot of different approaches as to how the high school head coach wanted his junior high teams to play. It was definitely apparent that some of the high school head coaches demanded more of their junior high teams than others, and maybe had more control as to what defenses and offenses were being taught.

What I saw was that the programs that had a system all the way down to the junior high schools were the most successful in the league. All of their teams from junior high to varsity, ran the same offenses and played the same defenses. However, there were only a handful of teams that did that.

It has always been my belief that youth teams should be taught man-to-man defense. Young players must be taught to defensive slide correctly, execute ball pressure, and learn all the individual and team defensive man-to-man principles. Only about half of the teams in our league did that. Many teams played some kind of zone, like a 1-3-1, 2-3, or 1-2-2. There is no doubt that your chances of winning at the junior high level are better if you play a zone defense, but you are really not teaching the defensive fundamentals that need to be taught. However, I have mellowed on this situation over the years. I do believe that playing some zone defense is permissible.

I think that probably some of the junior high coaches, even though they may be told to play man-to-man defense, disregard that in favor of trying to win the game with a zone defense. Playing zone is easier to teach and perimeter shooting at the junior high level is not that consistent so chances of winning are greater.

If I was a high school head coach I would demand that my junior high coaches teach my offense and my defense. If they did not, I would want to have an agreement with the junior high principal that they could be fired from their coaching position. But if the high school head coach has no interest in promoting his system then you have no worries. However, you are doing the players a disservice if you don't teach and play man-to-man defense.

That brings me to other youth coaches such as AAU, CYO, YMCA, etc. They should have the player's interests at heart and do everything they can do to develop those players and to get them ready to play at the next level. Man-to-man defense needs to be taught as well as the fundamentals of the game. It's not all about winning.

I saw the same emphasis on winning at the AAU level. Many of the AAU teams are "run-and-gun," play very little defense, and ignore teaching the fundamentals of the game. However, there were a few coaches that ran a disciplined program and made an attempt at teaching the fundamentals of the game. AAU just seemed to be all about playing, not really trying to teach the game.

## Six Minute Quarters And Fourteen Minute Halves

I mentioned earlier that I had to make a lot of adjustments coaching at the junior high level and AAU levels. One of those adjustments was getting used to the shorter playing minutes. Having coached at the college level for 36 years with the 20 minute halves, it was something I really couldn't get comfortable with.

The six minute quarters really had an effect on your substituting. The fourteen minute halves in AAU were a little bit better, but still difficult. The minutes went so fast that putting players into the game would pass me by. I finally started breaking the quarter into three two minute periods for junior high and three four and a half minutes for AAU. Doing that helped me greatly in making the proper substitutions.

In junior high, the situation that caused me problems was the understanding that when we got behind in the fourth quarter, there was not a whole lot of time left to make up the deficit. So getting behind going into the fourth quarter many times was impossible to overcome. But we did it a few times.

## Lack of An Assistant Coach

For the first time in my coaching career I didn't have an assistant coach. I coached the team entirely by myself both in practice and games. In practice, I couldn't break down and work with my big men or the guards. I tried to create ways that I could work with them in groups. The situation that worked best was to set up stations. I would set up four or five stations with different drills, and then rotate every few minutes. It wasn't the best situation, but it worked to some degree.

During games, I had no assistant to keep time outs and fouls on our team and the opponents. Most of the gyms we played in had old scoreboards and the number of fouls was not on the scoreboard. So I tried keeping it myself, but I would get involved in the game and miss a lot. Also, I had no assistant coach to keep statistics. Consequently, except for points scored and fouls committed, which was in the official scorebook, I had no stats.

If there is any way possible for you to have someone help you as an assistant coach, I would bring them on board. Even if it is a parent or a high school student. It definitely will make your life easier and I believe the players benefit tremendously.

## Parents

I didn't have many problems with parents. Most of the time the parents were appreciative of the job I was doing even though we did not win many games. However, I did have one situation in junior high where one of my players went to his parents and told them that I said I wished I had never taken the job and that I didn't like coaching them. Of course this was not true and it was something I did not say. I was very upset after one particular game because we had worked all week on how to properly defend the flex offense and we failed to do so during the game.

I got called in by the Athletic Director who told me about the parent complaint. I assured him I did not say those things, but told him I was very upset after the game and did say to the team that I was very disappointed in them.

I didn't seem to have many problems with parents coaching AAU. It seemed to be a little different atmosphere in terms of that situation. Things seemed to be more positive with how the parents looked at their child's AAU experience.

I think the key to dealing with parents is communication. At the junior high, I was fortunate that one of the parents volunteered to send out emails to all the other parents. I would notify the parent and she would send out emails. It really helped me immensely. I didn't want the parents to have any surprises. With players that age, taking them to practice and picking them up is crucial for the parents. I made sure that they knew of any changes in practice or games ahead of time.

With the AAU program the director of the program did most of the communicating with parents concerning practice and game times.

Certainly, parents complain about their son's or daughter's playing time. Fortunately none of the parents complained to me, the Athletic Director, or the AAU director about playing time. I did have a few players complain about the amount of time they were playing. I took them aside and told them the reasons why, but always told them how they could get more time.

However, I recognize that parents can be a very big problem. A very successful high school basketball coach in Michigan resigned because of parents. Clayton Castor who coached at Gladstone High School had this to say about his resignation, "At the end of the day, the reason I am resigning is because of parents. I don't want to deal with them. The last five years I have coached at Gladstone I have given it my life. My time could have been better spent doing other things. I really, really enjoy this, but parents have taken the fun and enjoyment right out of it. Maybe some of this is on me. I just don't have thick enough skin or the will to put up with it. For that amount of time, it's just not worth it."

## What Offense To Use?

This was covered more extensively in an earlier chapter. But I want to just mention some general items concerning my observations about offense at the junior high and AAU levels.

In junior high, probably 60% of the teams used some form of flex offense. All of the system type schools all used the flex offense. At both junior high and AAU, teams would run some form of ball screen offense, either a high ball screen or wing screen, sometimes both. A few teams ran "motion offense," but not many.

It seemed that teams that tried to run set plays, excluding the flex, turned the ball over quite frequently. I found with my teams that the players had difficulty carrying over things we did in practice, and particular with set plays we tried to execute.

There is no hesitation to say that the best philosophy on offense at the junior high and AAU is to Keep-It-Simple, and I mean very simple.

I learned that the attention span at the junior high for most of the players was not very long, so I would teach the offense in small doses in practice. However, there were a few players who had a great understanding of what we were trying to do on offense. What seemed to hurt the offense more than anything was the players whose fundamentals (dribbling and passing) were weak. They just couldn't execute the offense because of their lack of fundamentals. So again, there must be an emphasis on teaching fundamentals.

## Practice

Practice is mentioned in Chapter 7, but I wanted to give you my personal experience as to what practice was like at the junior high and AAU situation.

In junior high, we had two eighth grade boy's teams and we had to split the floor with the other eighth grade team. Both teams would come together in the last half hour and practice and scrimmage usually, so we did get in some full court work. But it certainly wasn't enough and I believe the teams suffered because of that situation. We could go sideways, which was full court, but not very long or wide. We pretty much had the same situation with the AAU team, not much full court practice time.

Consequently, I incorporated a system of always having them transit to half court. It wasn't the best but it got us thinking fast break and getting back on defense.

The biggest problem I had was in teaching position and spacing on offense, on the half court. It just wasn't the same when they came down to the offensive end on the full court. The players seemed to get lost and not know where to set up and then after one pass would be standing 5 feet from each other. I have always taught 15 to 18 foot spacing on offense. I think because of practicing on the half court the players had a hard time adjusting once we went to full court.

Conditioning was also a problem when you only practice on the half court. I made up several running drills and instituted running across the half court before we went on a water break called "17." The players had to touch each sideline 17 times in one minute. Certainly, full court work constantly in practice would have been much better.

Many coaches have limitations on their practices with either time or space. You can't use that as an excuse but just adjust and figure out what you can do.

My experience in coaching at the junior high level and the AAU was one of the most enjoyable and satisfying chapters of my coaching career. Seeing the players improve many times on a daily basis and experiencing their young spirit made it all worthwhile. And as I mentioned before, I developed a new respect for the coaches that coach at the younger player level. As always it's the Off-Broadway coach that gets overlooked, but in my heart, after this experience in junior high and AAU, many of those coaches were outstanding.

The following is information on several basketball organizations that offer play for both boys and girls:

*Amateur Athletic Union* (www.aauboysbasketball.org and www.aaugirlsbasketball.org)

Offers basketball competition from 7 years old to adult.

Sponsors local, regional and national competition.

*United States Basketball Association* (www.usbahoops.com)

Offers basketball competition for girls and boys from second grade to eleventh/twelfth grade.

Sponsors local, regional and national tournaments.

*United States Specialty Sports Association* (www.usssa.com)

Offers competition for boys, girls, and adults for 5 on 5 and 3 on 3 basketball.

Sponsors many types of basketball events at every age level.

# 25 A Little Touch of Broadway

In 1995, Rick Pitino, who was the head basketball coach at the University of Kentucky, decided that he was going to have a junior varsity team. The varsity team was very deep and talented and Pitino was looking for a way to get his freshmen on that team some experience and playing time.

So Nazr Mohammed, a 6-10 project at the time, Oliver Simmons, Jason Lathrem, and Cameron Mills were designated to play on the junior varsity along with Michael Yang, who made history by being the first UK basketball player of Asian descent. It also included Frank Vogel, who served as a student manager for the varsity team and later went on to coach the Indiana Pacers in the NBA. These players were allowed to play in varsity games as long as their total number of games did not exceed the NCAA limit. Coach Pitino decided that Delray Brooks would be the coach of the JV team.

A few months before that junior varsity team started playing games, we received a telephone call from the athletic department at the University of Kentucky asking if Cincinnati State would be interested in playing in a double header. The UK women's team would play Syracuse at 9 p.m. and Cincinnati State would play the UK Junior Varsity team at 7 p.m. at the Riverfront Coliseum, as it was called then. An incentive to buy a ticket to the double header was a ticket to the Kentucky vs. Vanderbilt game at the Riverfront Coliseum the next year. The tickets were sold for $30.

Of course we jumped at their proposal. Who would turn down an opportunity to play the University of Kentucky, even if it was their JV team? The date was set. We would play on Thursday, December 21, 1995.

The *Cincinnati Enquirer* reported the results of the game in the following manner: "'I'm in favor of winning every game,' said Delray Brooks, the basketball assistant coach who also runs Kentucky's new junior varsity team. He was making the point that while the JV program was set up by Rick Pitino to develop young players and keep varsity reserves in game shape, it matters—a lot—when they lose."

And when the Kentucky junior varsity lost to Cincinnati State 92–90 at Riverfront Stadium, Brooks said, "They wouldn't keep score if it didn't matter."

The audience of near 5,000 was mostly Kentucky fans, cheering their emerging players and ensuring their seats for the Kentucky–Vanderbilt varsity game next year at the Coliseum.

The Surge, without the seeming prowess of the Kentucky roster, fell behind by 11 points with less than 10 minutes in the game, and the result seemed a foregone conclusion.

But someone hadn't informed Andre Richardson, the State defensive star who came off the bench and created a number of UK turnovers, or Verdell Rawls, the former Aiken High star who

Nazr Mohammed

scored 34 points, including the six straight that put State five points ahead at the two-minute mark.

Kentucky's 6-10 Nazr Mohammed had fouled out at 3:09, finishing with 23 points and eight rebounds, and Brooks said losing their big guy wasn't an excuse but "it was a factor." I said it was a factor about as big as Mohammed himself, because guarding him tired everyone out.

Kentucky's leading scorer was Cameron Mills, a walk-on who won a varsity position but played with the JVs for the extra minutes. He had 25 points, and when he was asked about the difference between a varsity loss and a JV one, he said there wasn't any. "No different at all," he said, aggrieved. "You lose, you lose."

I remember after the game was over being called to come to the media room in Riverfront Coliseum to address the media. I got lost going to the room and showed up late and then just stood there for a few seconds, not knowing that I was first supposed to give my thoughts about the game before the media asked their questions. Well, after all it was my first taste of Broadway basketball.

Needless to say, playing against the University of Kentucky junior varsity team and beating them was a highlight of my career at Cincinnati State. The players and I all got a "little touch of Broadway basketball." Playing against players like Nazr Mohammed, who played 18 years in the NBA, and Cameron Mills, who would later in 1997 be the star of the NCAA tournament for the University of Kentucky, was such a dream for our players and our program.

# 26 Final Thoughts

The game of basketball has come a long way since Dr. James A. Naismith invented the game in 1891. He put "13 Basic Rules" together and the game grew to what we have now. Some think the game is not as good as it was in the past and others believe the game is much better with the rule changes that have occurred over the years. However, there is no argument that it is at the top of its popularity and that worldwide it has grown to the extent that it is second to only soccer throughout the world in popularity.

There is no doubt that players even at the lower levels are much better trained physically than they were in the past. Weight lifting, conditioning, and scientific approaches to physical improvement were not there in the past.

If there is one area of basketball that has evolved over the years, it is team and individual defensive play. Coaches at most levels understand the importance of teaching defense to their teams. And they understand that defense wins championships. It is much more difficult to score today than it was 25 years ago. Defense would be the equalizer to the great players of the past, compared to our great players of today.

The emphasis on young basketball talent is spiraling out of control. Exposure leagues and camps are popping up all over the United States. An organization known as "Junior Phenom" is having exposure camps for boys and girls from the second grade to the eighth grade. They rank players in a Top 100 list. I asked a prominent major college basketball coach a few years ago what would be the number one thing that I could do for him, and his reply was, "find out for me who the best 12 year olds are in the area."

Of course AAU basketball is as big as any enterprise we have going today. Both boys and girls teams start at the eighth grade level and go on up to high school. There are thousands of teams in the United States. Usually play starts after the high school season is over and goes into the summer. Numerous tournaments are held in each state, usually on the weekends and can lead to participation at the national level. AAU has become a very important part in college recruiting. College coaches have switched the majority of their recruiting to the AAU games and the high school season becomes secondary in their efforts.

For many young basketball players, the season becomes a twelve month venture. If they play basketball at a school, play AAU basketball, participate in camps, either exposure or skill, it becomes a very long season. There is not much time for the young athlete to play other sports. It has been debated over the years about what is best for the young athlete, to play one sport or to try several sports.

In my opinion, we have lost something in all of this. I am not sure the players are better that go through this twelve month season. I think that there are certain things that are not being taught to the young athlete, from fundamentals to character traits. I absolutely believe that there is an overemphasis on winning. Ideas that coaches in the past have tried to teach to players such as discipline, teamwork, fundamentals, leadership, doing things correctly, integrity, and being the best that you can be have become second-rate.

One of the areas that we see such a disparity in is in the area of teamwork. When our teams play at the world level, we usually see that the teams from other countries execute teamwork much more than our U.S. teams. Our teams are more 1-on-1, and sometimes selfish with the basketball. Shot selection is poor and the possession of the basketball is not appreciated.

So…you as the new coach have a great opportunity to coach the right way. I believe it is a fact that coaches today are not as respected as they once were. You have that chance to build that solid reputation for yourself. But you must understand that this is something that you must earn. Integrity is the key word in everything that you do. If you are going to build that reputation, this should never be slighted.

As the coach, no matter at what level, you must be a leader and role model, even if you don't want to be. Next to the parents, you are very important in the development of this young person. You must be a teacher, first and foremost. And you must look upon yourself in that manner. You must understand that the things you teach about life are more important than what you teach about basketball.

One of the most important traits for the new basketball coach to develop should be the ability to adapt. I always felt that this was my biggest asset. I was able to figure it out and change if I had to. I believe it was the sole reason for my success. I never got frustrated or made excuses or complained, no matter what the situation. John Wooden, in his book *Practical Modern Basketball*, stated that, "after he quit complaining about UCLA's lack of facilities and adapted to what he had, he began to win national championships." What I found out is that there is always a way.

I always remember one of the things my high school coach told me. He said, "that he always wanted to make basketball so enjoyable for the player that if that player ever had a choice to play another sport or get into another activity, that the player would choose basketball above everything else."

Basketball is such a tremendous and exciting game. I love just to hear the sneakers screeching on the hardwood, the smell of the gym, the sound of the balls bouncing on the floor, the popcorn, and the coaches whistle. I hope you are as excited about the game as I am, no matter what level you might be coaching. I hope this book has helped you and that you have what I didn't have when I started coaching basketball, and that is that you have some idea of how to coach this great game!

"It's what you learn after you know it all that matters most."
—John Wooden

# Common Basketball Terminology

*Arm bar:* The action of using the forearm to body check an offensive player.

*Ball side:* This refers to the side of the floor where the ball is located.

*Close out:* This refers to the method in which a defender quickly slides up to and contests a possible shooter.

*Deny:* The defensive play that prevents an offensive player from receiving the ball.

*Entry pass:* A pass made to initiate the offense.

*Give & Go:* A very basic play where after passing to a teammate, the passer quickly cuts toward the basket and receives the return pass.

*Help & Recover:* The defensive action of simulating a switch on a pick and then retreating back to the offensive player.

*Help side:* The opposite side away from the ball.

*High Post:* That area along the free throw line and both "elbows."

*Low Post:* The area near the "block" on either side of the lane, to about half way up the lane toward the free throw line.

*On the line:* Your defensive position is such that you can see your man and the ball, and your body is on that imaginary line.

*Outlet pass:* A pass thrown by a rebound that initiates the fast break.

*Pick & Roll:* A play where an offensive player sets a screen on a dribbling teammate's defender, thereby freeing up the teammate, after which the screener moves or rolls to the basket for a return pass.

*Point:* Out front, around the top of the key area.

*Reverse the ball:* Moving the ball side-top-side, move ball to the opposite wing.

*Screen:* When an offensive player intentionally blocks the path of a defender.

*Skip pass:* A cross-court pass.

*Step & Go:* A backdoor cut, executed by stepping toward the ball and then planting the outside foot and going backdoor.

*Up the line:* When you are in a position away from your man/girl, located toward the ball.

*V cut:* Taking your man/girl on offense in the opposite direction and then cutting back toward the ball in a "V" type motion.

# Players John Hurley Coached Who Went on to 4-Year Colleges from Cincinnati State (2-Year College)

| | | |
|---|---|---|
| *1978–79* | Mike Brown | Heidelberg College |
| | Greg Crutcher | University of Montana |
| | Bryan Clark | Pro BB: Switzerland |
| *1979–80* | Victor Hunter | Milligan University |
| | Paul Jones | Xavier University |
| *1980–81* | Rory Glasco | Indiana State |
| | Phil Davis | Central Arkansas |
| *1981–82* | Tony Williams | Central State University |
| *1982–83* | George Chea | Central State University |
| | Adair Carmichael | Central State University |
| | Cam Houston | Southern Tech |
| | Gary Dennis | Southern Tech |
| *1983–84* | Mark Parker | Indiana Tech |
| | Gerald Mann | Paine College |
| *1984–85* | Mike Bogan | Paine College |
| | Gerald Booker | Limestone College |
| *1985–86* | David Wagner | Iona University |
| | Scott Calcatera | N.W. Missouri State |
| | Dave Remenowsky | Walsh College |

| | | |
|---|---|---|
| *1986–87* | Glen Hughes | Earlham College |
| | Terry Roberson | Ferris State |
| *1987–88* | Jerry Moore | Thomas More |
| | Ron Benford | Northern Kentucky University |
| | Sean Mason | Walsh College |
| | Craig Latcha | Milligan College |
| | Britton Jackson | Shawnee State |
| *1988–89* | Orlando Williams | University of Cincinnati |
| *1989–90* | Fritz Taylor | Christian Bros. |
| | Chris Williams | University of California/Pennsylvania |
| | Ray Lawson | Shawnee State |
| *1990–91* | Brian Kelly | Georgetown University (Hoyas) |
| | Gary Wehrum | Arkansas State |
| | Mike Eubanks | University of New Orleans |
| | Renfred Davis | Tuskegee University |
| | Kevin Pace | Shawnee State |
| *1991–92* | Mark Allen | Indiana/Purdue Ft. Wayne |
| | Trent Martin | Carroll College |
| *1992–93* | Matt Reicheneker | Pan American University |
| | Sam Byrd | Indiana/Purdue Indy. |
| *1993–94* | Willis Thompson | University of Charleston (West Virginia) |
| | Todd Gray | University of Charleston (West Virginia) |
| | Liori Kennedy | Central State University |
| | Mike Davis | Clark University |
| | Tyrone Bradford | Clark University |
| | Jason Blom | Roberts Wesleyan/Pro BB: Ireland |
| *1994–95* | James Newman | Memphis University |
| | John Miller | Tiffin University |
| | Antonio McCants | West Virginia Wesleyan |

| | | |
|---|---|---|
| *1995–96* | Tommy Feagin | Salem Teikyo University |
| | Mark Hughes | Salem Teikyo University |
| | Rick Rushing | Hannibal LaGrange |
| *1996–97* | Chris Haynes | Armstrong State |
| | Seneca Herring | Rio Grande University |
| | Marcus Johnson | Central Methodist |
| | Andre Richardson | Tiffin University |
| *1997–98* | Adrian Stockman | Winthrop University |
| | Courtnay Tolliver | Alderson Broaddus |
| *1998–99* | Quentin Smith | Morehead University |
| | Joe Rivers | West Virginia State University |
| | Roberto Allen | Ohio Dominican |
| *1999–00* | Sylvester Allen | IUPUI |
| | Maurice Williams | IUPUI |
| | Jamal Mills | Norfolk State |
| | Sam McIntyre | Missouri Valley |
| | Tony Taylor | Fayetteville State |
| *2000–01* | Lamont Speaks | Western Carolina |
| | Baboucarr Njie | Indiana/Purdue Ft. Wayne |
| | Bakary Konate | Bowie State University |
| *2001–02* | Belco Bamba | Florida International |
| | Mike Kuhn | Hampton University |
| *2002–03* | Jason Hauck | Taylor University |
| | Damon Francis | Ouachita University |
| | Malcolm Manier | Georgia State |

# Players John Hurley Coached Who Transferred
## from U.C. Clermont College

| | | |
|---|---|---|
| *2004–05* | Troy Girty | Bluefield College (Virginia) |
| | Justin Phillips | Shawnee State |
| *2005–06* | Michael Holmes | Brevard College (North Carolina) |
| *2006–07* | Brad Hosler | Northern Kentucky University |
| | Maurice Brown | University of the Cumberlands |
| *2009–10* | Kraig Unger | Shawnee State University |
| *2010–11* | A.D. Graves | Harlem Globetrotters/Pro BB: China |
| *2011–12* | Tyler Knabb | Wilmington College |
| | Clint Boring | Ohio Dominican University |

# NCAA Statistics Services 6-Year Study of Division I Trends

Here are the final 2015 national totals and per team/per game averages for Division I men's basketball. The final 2010, 2011, 2012, 2013, and 2014 seasons are also included for comparison.

| | *Final 2010* | *Final 2011* | *Final 2012* | *Final 2013* | *Final 2014* | *Final 2015* |
|---|---|---|---|---|---|---|
| *Teams* | 334 | 335 | 338 | 345 | 345 | 345 |
| *Games* | 32.21 | 32.32 | 32.46 | 32.53 | 32.69 | 33.13 |
| *FGM* | 24.28 | 24.14 | 23.97 | 23.82 | 24.52 | 23.64 |
| *FGA* | 55.71 | 55.28 | 54.96 | 55.00 | 55.41 | 54.34 |
| *FG%* | 43.58% | 43.66% | 43.60% | 43.30% | 44.24% | 43.49% |
| *3FGM* | 6.25 | 6.27 | 6.22 | 6.17 | 6.30 | 6.41 |
| *3FGA* | 18.20 | 18.16 | 18.07 | 18.12 | 18.20 | 18.58 |
| *3FG%* | 34.33% | 34.53% | 34.42% | 34.05% | 34.61% | 34.51% |
| *2FGM* | 18.03 | 17.87 | 17.75 | 17.65 | 18.22 | 17.21 |
| *2FGA* | 37.51 | 37.12 | 36.89 | 36.88 | 37.21 | 35.66 |
| *2FG%* | 48.06% | 48.13% | 48.10% | 47.85% | 48.96% | 48.26% |
| *FTM* | 14.48 | 14.50 | 13.86 | 13.70 | 15.66 | 13.95 |
| *FTA* | 21.01 | 20.94 | 20.06 | 19.76 | 22.44 | 20.16 |
| *FT%* | 68.92% | 69.26% | 69.10% | 69.31% | 69.79% | 69.22% |
| *Points* | 69.30 | 69.05 | 68.01 | 67.50 | 71.00 | 67.74 |
| *Personal Fouls* | 18.56 | 18.73 | 18.07 | 17.68 | 19.11 | 18.20 |
| *Rebounds* | 35.17 | 34.83 | 34.48 | 34.57 | 34.81 | 34.29 |
| *Assists* | 13.07 | 13.02 | 12.89 | 12.82 | 12.75 | 12.62 |
| *Blocked Shots* | 3.49 | 3.45 | 3.43 | 3.48 | 3.66 | 3.48 |
| *Steals* | 6.72 | 6.46 | 6.55 | 6.71 | 6.18 | 6.27 |
| *Turnovers* | 13.66 | 13.47 | 13.46 | 13.30 | 12.30 | 12.52 |

# Most College Basketball Coaches' Wins of All-Time

## USA Today, October 2012

| | | | |
|---|---|---|---|
| 1. | Harry Statham | 1,068 | *McKendree College* |
| 2. | Danny Miles | 987 | *Oregon Tech* |
| 3. | Herb Magee | 960 | *Philadelphia College* |
| 4. | Mike Krzyzewski | 957 | *Army & Duke University* |
| 5. | John Hurley | 923 | *Cincinnati State & UC Clermont* |
| 5. | Don Meyer | 923 | *Lipscomb College* |

# Hurley's System

| *System Item* | *Subject* | *Website* |
|---|---|---|
| Press Offense | Full Court Zone Press Attack | www.hoopsu.com |
| Numbered Fast Break | Fastbreak Transition | www.coachesclipboard.net |
| Motion Offense | 2-Rule Motion Offense | www.coachingbetterbball.blogspot.com |
| 1-3-1 Zone Offense | 1-3-1 Zone Offense | www.hoopsplus.org |
| Man to Man Defense | Basic Man to Man Defense | www.coachesclipboard.net |
| 2-3 Zone Defense | Syracuse 2-3 Zone Defense | www.coachingtoolbox.net |
| Out of Bounds Plays | 1-4 Baseline Out of Bounds | www.coachpintar.com |
| Half Court Trap Offense | Trap Continuity Offense | www.hoopsu.com |

This chart was designed to show you how you can use the internet to help you coach your team. If you go to the web site and plug in the subject you will get all the information about that subject that you will want to know. If you Google the subject then you can even learn more about the particular subject.

The system that I have outlined for you in the above chart is my recommendation for what a young coach should think about including into his/her offensive and defensive system. You could add or delete from my ideas. I have explained earlier in Chapter 22 why I chose these particular items in my system.

As has been explained in earlier chapters, you can virtually find anything about coaching basketball on the internet. There are not many secrets in the game of basketball. You will be able to find all of the offenses and defenses that are being used today and the ones used in the past.

As I have mentioned before, I did not have the luxury of having the internet to use in helping me get started as a basketball coach. It would not be very smart for a basketball coach to ignore all this information that is available at your fingertips on the internet.

If you have any questions, please feel free to contact me at johnehurley@yahoo.com.

# About the Author

JOHN HURLEY was born in Portsmouth, Ohio, and concluded his college head coaching career at UC Clermont in 2014. He previously coached at Cincinnati State where he recorded 554 wins and presently has 923 career victories, which is ranked 5th all-time in college basketball. He is tied 5th with Don Meyer, legendary coach at Lipscomb College. He was inducted into the National Junior College Athletic Association Basketball Coaches "Hall of Fame" in 2004. In 2012, he was recognized by the National Association of Basketball Coaches for his 900th career win. Hurley has averaged 22.6 wins per season as a head coach.

In 2004, he accepted an offer to coach at the University of Cincinnati Clermont where he won a National Championship in 2007.

*Playing Career*

Hurley, who grew up in Portsmouth, Ohio, played basketball for legendary high school basketball coach George Heller. Hurley was recruited to play college basketball at Bowling Green State University, where he had an injury-plagued career. During his four years there, Bowling Green recorded the best records in the history of the basketball program, with such players as Howard Komives and Nate Thurmond.

*Coaching Career*

Hurley launched his coaching career as a graduate assistant at Ohio University. He then had stints at Antwerp, Defiance, and Milford high schools as head basketball coach.

*Cincinnati State (1977–2004)*

Hurley started the intercollegiate men's basketball program at Cincinnati State in 1977. While at Cincinnati State he recorded 554 wins. He won fifteen league championships, and twelve tournament championships in the Ohio Community College Athletic Conference. He also won four regional championships in 1990, 1992, 2000, and 2003. He was named Ohio Community College coach of the year and regional coach of the year several times. In 2009, Hurley was the first inductee into the Cincinnati State Technical and Community College "Athletic Hall of Fame."

*University of Cincinnati Clermont (2004–2013)*

Hurley announced in 2004 that he had accepted the position of head coach at the UC Clermont. He immediately won 20 games and was runner-up in the Ohio Regional Campus Athletic Conference following an eight win season the year before. Several conference and conference tournament championships have followed, but with the joining of the United State Collegiate Athletic Association in 2005 UC Clermont has had national recognition during Hurley's tenure. In 2007 Hurley's team won the National Championship.

*Player Development*

Hurley has been known as a great recruiter and has taken players who had potential and developed them into college players. While at Cincinnati State he had 65 players receive athletic scholarships from NAIA to NCAA Division I colleges.

*Other Accomplishments*

Author of several published basketball coaching articles of which one on "Shot Discipline" appears in the book *Coaching Basketball* by Jerry Krause. Hurley's article is there with Bob Knight, Dean Smith, Adolph Rupp, Rick Pitino, John Wooden and others.

Was selected in 2008 to run the National Association of Basketball Coaches "Skills Champ" basketball camps.

*Coaching Honors and Awards*

Member of the Ohio High School Basketball Coaches Association "Hall of Fame," for winning 100 high school games, inducted in 1975.

Member of the National Junior College Athletic Association Coaches "Hall of Fame" inducted in 2004.

Recently recognized by the National Association of Basketball Coaches for milestone of 900 victories.

First inductee into Cincinnati State Technical and Community College "Athletic Hall of Fame" in 2009.

"Coach of the Year" honors in the Ohio Community College Athletic Conference, 1986, 1987, 1990, 1992, 1995, 1997, 2000, 2001, and 2003.

Coach of the Year: honors in the NJCAA Region XII, 1990, 1992, 2000, and 2003.

Coach of the Year: honors for the Ohio Collegiate Athletic Conference in 2010, 2011, and 2012.

Inducted into the Portsmouth High School Athletic "Hall of Fame" in September of 2012.

Member of the Greater Cincinnati Basketball "Hall of Fame," inducted in 2011.

# Bibliography

## Books

Bilas, Jay, *Toughness Developing True Strength On and Off the Court,* Berkley Press, March 4, 2014.

Foran, Bill and Pound, Robin, *Complete Conditioning for Basketball,* Human Kinetics Publishers, 3rd edition, August 1, 2007.

Jucker, Ed, *Cincinnati Power Basketball,* Prentice-Hall, 1st edition 1962.

Krzyzewski, Mike, *The Gold Standard: Building a World-Class Team,* Hatchette, Mar 27, 2009.

McCormick, Brian, *The 21st Century Basketball Practice; Modernizing the basketball practice to develop the global player.* 180Shooter.com, Nov 12, 2014.

Mackay, Harvey, *We Got Fired and It's the Best Thing that Happened to Us,* Ballantine Books, September 28, 2004.

Musselman, Bill, *33.9 Defense,* 1969.

Riley, Pat, *The Winner Within; A Life Plan for Team Players,* Berkley Press, October 1, 1994.

Smith, Dean. *Basketball Multiple Offense and Defense,* Benjamin Cummings, First edition December 8, 1998.

Wooden, John, *Practical Modern Basketball,* Pearson 2nd edition, March 5, 1993.

## Articles

Crookes. Complan Column, *Athletics Coach,* 1991

Baumgartner, Greg. *Daddy Ball: The Painful Reality,* www.ezinearticles.com, July 31, 2010

Kelbrick, Don. *Getting your Basketball Team to Play Hard,* www.drillzandskillz-basketball.com, 2017

James, Jon. *Daddy Ball: What it is and How to Avoid It,* www.spidersite.com, 2016

McLean, Trevor. *How to Easily Stop Selfishness in Basketball,* www.basketball-forcoaches.com

Moody, Craig. *Learning to Play Hard: The Number One Skill in Basketball,* www.shoot360.com, November 13, 2014

Ulloa-Colina, Constanza. *How to Deal With Daddy Ball,* www.ripit.com, July 22, 2015

## Websites

Brown, Hubie. June 2017. www.hoopsplaybook.ca

Carrier, John. March 2017. www.coachingbasketball.com

Ekker, Ron. April 2017. www.basketballtalkpro.com

Frabritz, Paul. June 2017. www.stack.com

Hanson, Tom. December 2016. www.webball.com

Hueffner, John. July 2017. www.breakthroughbasketball.com

Lehmann, George. July 2017. www.youtube.com

Mahoney, Rob. April 2017. www.SI.com

Robichaux, Tony. April 2017. www.pressprosmagazine.com

Willams, Brian. May 2017. www.coachingtoolbox.net

May 2017. www.universityofwisconsinhealthandsportsmedicine.com

May 2017. www.kidshealth.com